creating
a web video
in silverlight

Visual QuickProject Guide

by Bruce Hyslop

Peachpit
Press

Visual QuickProject Guide
Creating a Web Video in Silverlight
Bruce Hyslop

Peachpit Press

1249 Eighth Street
Berkeley, CA 94710
510/524-2178
800/283-9444
510/524-2221 (fax)

Find us on the World Wide Web at: www.peachpit.com
To report errors, please send a note to errata@peachpit.com
Peachpit Press is a division of Pearson Education

Editor: Clifford Colby
Production Coordinator: Becky Winter
Compositor: Rick Gordon, Emerald Valley Graphics
Cover design: The Visual Group with Aren Howell
Cover production: Charlene Will
Cover photo credit: Mark Evans/iStockphoto.com
Interior design: Elizabeth Castro
Indexer: Julie Bess

Notice of Rights

Notice of Liability

Trademarks

ISBN 13: 978-0-321-55422-2
ISBN 10: 0-321-55422-1

9 8 7 6 5 4 3 2 1

Printed and bound in the United States of America

To family both here and not.
To Mari.

Special Thanks to...

Clifford Colby. I can't imagine having a better, more patient, or more fun editor with whom to work.

Becky Winter for helping us stay on track.

Rick Gordon for assisting me with image prep and for turning around layouts quickly.

Everyone else at Peachpit for both the opportunity and for your part in making this book a reality.

Robert Reinhardt, the Man-Who-Spawned-a-Thousand-Technical-Writers, for his generosity in recommending me for this effort.

Agnes Liu, the ultratalented, for creating the OnTheGoFootage design and incorporating changes along the way.

David Sayed, Wayne Smith, James Clarke, and Randy Oakley of Microsoft for providing the inside scoop.

contents

contents

contents

introduction

The Visual QuickProject Guide that you hold in your hands offers a unique way to learn about new technologies. Instead of drowning you in theoretical possibilities and lengthy explanations, this Visual QuickProject Guide uses big, color illustrations coupled with clear, concise step-by-step instructions to show you how to complete one specific project in a matter of hours.

Our project in this book is to create a Web site that uses a Silverlight 2 video player you will output as part of learning how to enhance and encode videos with Microsoft Expression Encoder 2. You will also learn several best practices related to building sites. Our site is for the fictitious OnTheGoFootage, which features both user-generated and submitted videos documenting their travel adventures. However, the skills you will learn along the way both in terms of how to use Encoder and incorporate the Silverlight player into a site can be applied to any site for which you would like to feature high-quality video in a usable interface.

what you'll create

These two pages indicate just some of what you will learn and create.

Add a leader and trailer.

Create a custom encoding profile.

Crop your video.

Import your video.

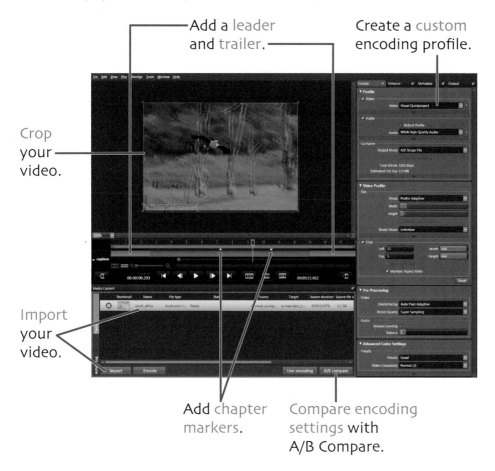

Add chapter markers.

Compare encoding settings with A/B Compare.

Incorporate a Silverlight 2 video player outputted from Encoder.

Add video captions.

Create a list of more videos available on the site, and build additional pages to showcase them.

Add a video overlay.

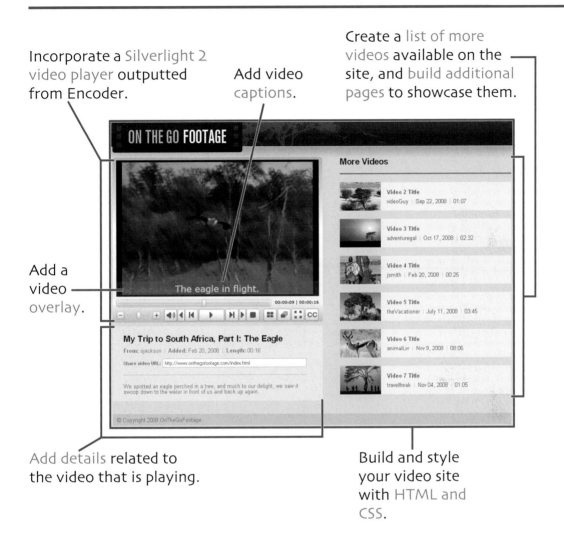

ON THE GO FOOTAGE

The eagle in flight.

00:00:09 | 00:00:16

CC

My Trip to South Africa, Part I: The Eagle

From: sjackson | Added: Feb 20, 2008 | Length: 00:16

Share video URL: http://www.onthegofootage.com/index.html

We spotted an eagle perched in a tree, and much to our delight, we saw it swoop down to the water in front of us and back up again.

© Copyright 2008 OnTheGoFootage

More Videos

Video 2 Title
videoGuy | Sep 22, 2008 | 01:07

Video 3 Title
adventuregal | Oct 17, 2008 | 02:32

Video 4 Title
jsmith | Feb 20, 2008 | 00:25

Video 5 Title
theVacationer | July 11, 2008 | 03:45

Video 6 Title
animalLvr | Nov 9, 2008 | 08:06

Video 7 Title
travelfreak | Nov 04, 2008 | 01:05

Add details related to the video that is playing.

Build and style your video site with HTML and CSS.

how this book works

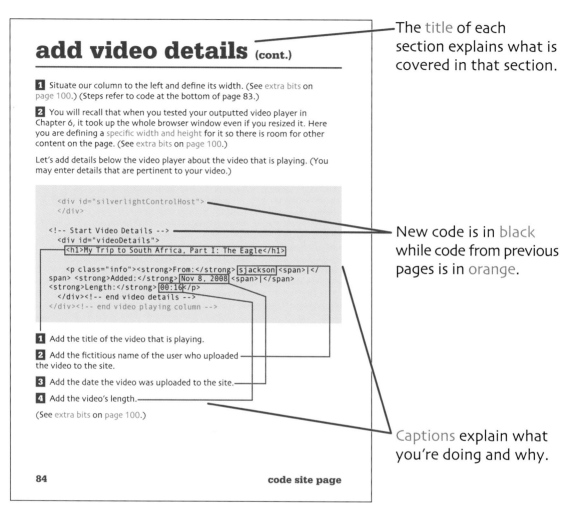

The title of each section explains what is covered in that section.

add video details (cont.)

1 Situate our column to the left and define its width. (See extra bits on page 100.) (Steps refer to code at the bottom of page 83.)

2 You will recall that when you tested your outputted video player in Chapter 6, it took up the whole browser window even if you resized it. Here you are defining a specific width and height for it so there is room for other content on the page. (See extra bits on page 100.)

Let's add details below the video player about the video that is playing. (You may enter details that are pertinent to your video.)

```
<div id="silverlightControlHost">
</div>

<!-- Start Video Details -->
<div id="videoDetails">
<h1>My Trip to South Africa, Part I: The Eagle</h1>

    <p class="info"><strong>From:</strong> sjackson <span>|</
span> <strong>Added:</strong> Nov 8, 2008 <span>|</span>
<strong>Length:</strong> 00:16</p>
    </div><!-- end video details -->
</div><!-- end video playing column -->
```

New code is in black while code from previous pages is in orange.

1 Add the title of the video that is playing.

2 Add the fictitious name of the user who uploaded the video to the site.

3 Add the date the video was uploaded to the site.

4 Add the video's length.

(See extra bits on page 100.)

Captions explain what you're doing and why.

84   code site page

A screenshot shows the effect of the new code in the browser.

My Trip to South Africa, Part I: The Eagle

From: sjackson | Added: Feb 20, 2008 | Length: 00:16

introduction

The extra bits section at the end of chapters contains additional tips and tricks that you might like to know but that aren't absolutely necessary for creating the project.

The heading for each group of tips matches the section title. (The colors are just for decoration and have no hidden meaning.)

Next to the heading there's a page number that also shows which section the tips belong to.

extra bits

gather assets p. 74

- It is a best practice not to repeat the image type (thumb, in this case) in the file name if its folder name represents the same. In other words, it is redundant to have a thumb_ image in a thumb folder. However, we've done so here to be explicit and make the code example a little easier to follow.

start HTML page p. 76

- We are using the XHTML 1.0 Strict DOCTYPE for our code. The W3C provides a service at http:// validator.w3.org/#validate-by-upload to help you make sure your code is valid. Invalid code often still works, but it is a good practice to validate your code, and it may help you catch any typing errors during our exercise. It should be noted once you put the video player object code from Encoder into your page later in this chapter, your code will no longer validate. That is OK in this instance. For more information about XHTML 1.0, consult http:// www.w3.org/TR/xhtml1/ or an HTML reference.

start style sheet p. 78

- Whereas HTML provides the content for a page, CSS dictates the presentation. You may have seen CSS placed inline in HTML, but it is a best practice to keep content and presentation separated in the manner we are doing.

- Web browsers have default style settings (such as margins and padding) on various HTML elements. However, they aren't always consistent from one browser to the next. A CSS Reset is a CSS rule or series of rules aimed at establishing a consistent baseline amongst browsers upon which you can then build your page. We are using a simplified version of Eric Meyer's CSS Reset (see http://meyerweb.com/eric/ thoughts/2007/05/01/reset-reloaded/). This is just one of a few approaches, though his is one of the most widely adopted. Perform a search for css resets if you are interested in seeing more.

code site page

companion web site

The companion Web site for Creating a Web Video in Silverlight is located at www.peachpit.com/silverlightvqj.

The site contains a file for you to download called silverlightvqj.zip. It contains several files you will need to complete the project.

You can also download the files that make up the final project site.

Lastly, you can find any updated material or corrections to mistakes.

what you'll need

You will need a few tools and files to begin your project:

- Microsoft Expression Encoder 2 with Service Pack 1 (SP1)—Encoder is the tool you will use to enhance and encode videos, and export a Silverlight 2 video player. Encoder SP1 is required since previous versions of Encoder had fewer features and only outputted Silverlight 1-compatible video players. While Encoder itself is not free, if you have version 2 then SP1 can be downloaded for free at http://www.microsoft.com/downloads/details.aspx?FamilyId=A29BE9F9-29E1-4E70-BF67-02D87D3E556E&displaylang=en. (If you do not want to type that URL, a link to it is accessible from http://www.microsoft.com/expression/try-it/Default.aspx?filter=servicepacks.)

- A text editor for writing HTML and CSS. See extra bits in Chapter 7 on page 72 for a little more guidance if you aren't sure what to use.

- The project assets ZIP file located on the companion Web site (see the previous section). Before you get started, download the file and extract the contents onto your hard drive.

- At least one video file. Neither the quality nor nature of content is important, as you will be using it primarily as a means to learn. However, it's best if the file is neither too short (under 20–30 seconds) nor too long (more than a minute). The longer the video, the longer it takes Encoder to encode it, which could slow down your progress during the book.

If you are having a hard time locating a video, do a search on your computer for *.wmv, which would find any video that has a file name ending in .wmv.

Once you have determined the file you would like to use, copy it and then go to the location where you extracted the companion site ZIP file. Navigate to the visual_quickproject/assets/unencoded_video folder and paste your video inside it.

See extra bits in Chapter 1 on page 10 for more information about what video file formats Encoder can import.

the next step

While this Visual QuickProject Guide will give you an excellent foundation in creating Web videos in Silverlight, you don't have to stop here if you want to take full advantage of Microsoft's design and development tools.

If you are curious, check out two other books by Peachpit Press: Microsoft Expression Blend 2 for Windows: Visual QuickStart Guide by Corey Schuman and Robert Reinhardt and Microsoft Expression Web 2 for Windows: Visual QuickStart Guide by Nolan Hester.

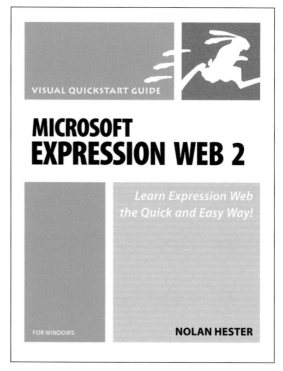

1. welcome to encoder

Expression Encoder 2 is rich with features for both adjusting and encoding video. In addition, it allows you to export your video with a fully functional Silverlight video player that you can use on your Web site.

In this book, you will learn about many of these features as we progress through the project. Soon enough, you'll see just how easy Encoder is to use.

But before we begin, let's get comfortable with Encoder's interface and learn how to customize it according to our preferences.

Main menu   Media Player panel

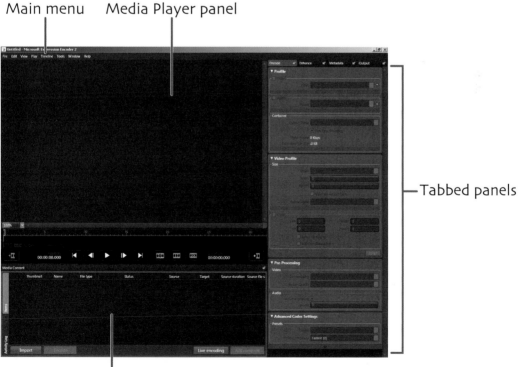

Tabbed panels

Media Content panel

explore encoder

The main menu contains several options, most of which are also available to you elsewhere in the application. Furthermore, as is typical of Windows applications, you can perform many of the commands on menus via keyboard shortcuts, displayed to the right of the command. (See extra bits on page 10.)

All told, you can perform the same action in a variety of ways, according to your preference.

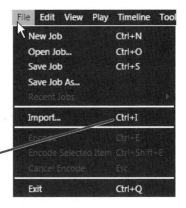

The Media Player panel displays the video with which you are working, along with the timeline, transport controls, and other features.

The Media Content panel lists the videos currently imported into Encoder and which will be part of any job output you perform.

Tab headers

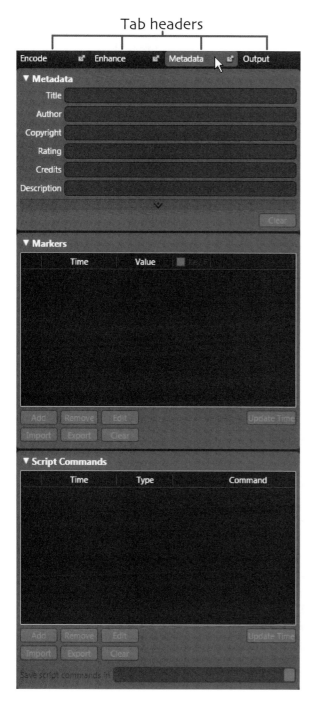

The tabbed panels provide a variety of options for adjusting and exporting your video. Clicking one of the four tab headers reveals that panel's options.

(See extra bits on page 10.)

welcome to encoder

import video

To work with a video, you must, of course, first load it into Encoder. (See extra bits on page 10.)

Import

1 Click the Import button. (Alternatively, you can use File > Import to perform the same action.)

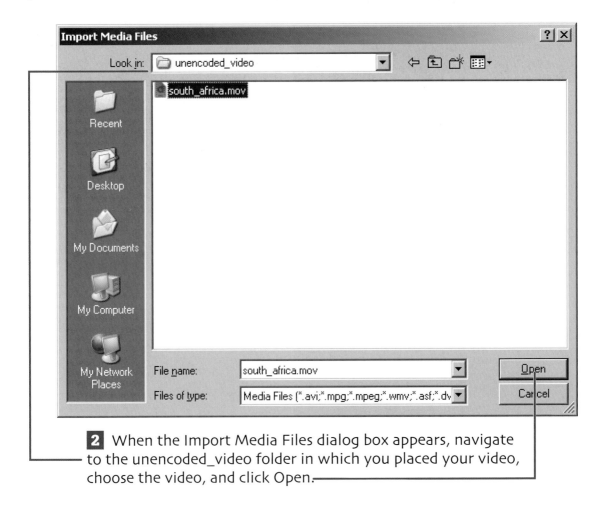

2 When the Import Media Files dialog box appears, navigate to the unencoded_video folder in which you placed your video, choose the video, and click Open.

It may take Encoder a few seconds to analyze, but soon the video you selected should appear in the Media Player panel and is listed in the Media Content panel along with information about the video. (See extra bits on page 10.)

Remove button   Column bar

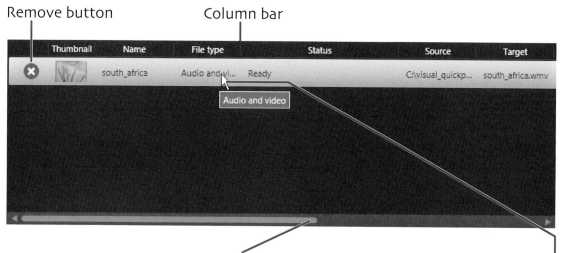

You may need to scroll to the right to view some of these details, such as the Source dimensions and Source frame rate.

Also, some values may be too long to fit in a column. If so, you can view the entire value either by dragging the column bar or hovering over the value. (See extra bits on page 10.)

If you opened the wrong video, remove it from your Encoder job by clicking the Remove button, which, as shown above, is the X to the left of the video thumbnail.

play video

Now that we've imported a video, we can play it in Encoder using the transport controls.

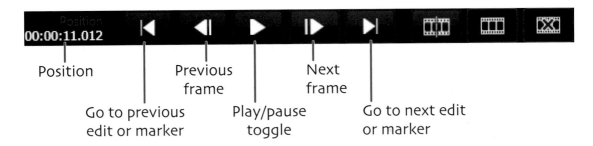

Position — Previous frame — Next frame

Go to previous edit or marker — Play/pause toggle — Go to next edit or marker

The functionality of most of these is self-explanatory, with the possible exception of the buttons allowing you to move to an edit or marker. We will cover these in greater depth in later chapters.

Click the Play button and notice how the Position value changes as the video advances.

The Timeline is a visual representation in seconds (and fractions thereof) of the video. Similar to the Position value, the playhead indicates the point on the timeline at which the video is playing or paused. You can drag the playhead to move to any point in the video (it's usually easier to do this when the video is paused).

Another way to jump to a specific point of the video is to click the Position value and edit it manually.

(See extra bits on page 11 if you are experiencing playback problems.)

customize workspace

What we've seen so far is Encoder's default layout. However, you can modify it to your liking.

One way to do this is to float a panel, allowing you to drag it anywhere on the screen or even to a second monitor if you have one. Each panel that can be floated has a Float button. As such, the Media Content panel and all of the tabbed panels can be floated.

You can resize a floated panel by dragging its bottom-right corner.

When you float a panel, the float button changes to a Dock button. Click this button to return the panel to its default location.

customize workspace (cont.)

You can resize a docked panel by dragging its edge. All other panels will resize accordingly.

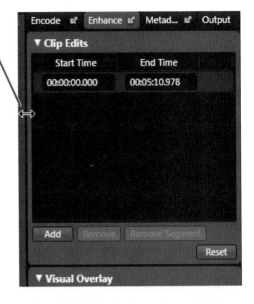

Another way to modify the look of Encoder is to collapse a module (also called a category) within a panel in one of the tabs. The module toggles between open and closed modes by clicking on the module's header. This is handy if you prefer to minimize the amount of visual noise on your workspace. You can have more than one module collapsed at a time.

The workspace zoom feature allows you to enlarge or shrink the entire interface. Select Tools > Options from the main menu to display the Options dialog box.

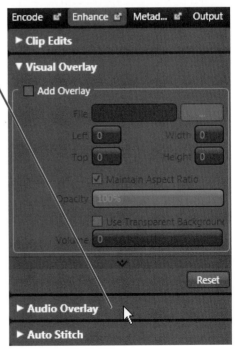

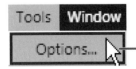

welcome to encoder

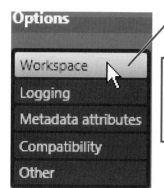

Within that, select Workspace at left (it may already be selected for you). You may then drag the Workspace zoom bar with your mouse or click it to edit the value manually. (See extra bits on page 11.) The interface will adjust as a preview, but you must click the OK button to enact the change.

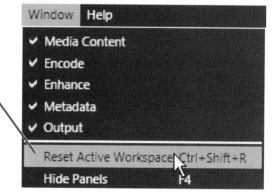

Give all these options a try to see what Encoder configuration you most prefer. At any point you can use Window > Reset Active Workspace to return the entire interface to its default layout. (See extra bits on page 11.)

For the purposes of this book, we will use the default layout configuration.

extra bits

explore encoder p. 2

- A complete list of keyboard shortcuts is available in the Encoder User Guide under References and other resources > Keyboard shortcuts > Main workspace shortcuts. You can print the list from the guide to keep it as a reference.

- The User Guide can be found in the main menu under Help > User Guide or by hitting F1 on your keyboard. The guide provides helpful descriptions of Encoder's features, sometimes in more depth than shown here. For instance, more information about the interface options are available in the guide's section entitled "The workspace."

- Depending on your screen resolution and how you have sized your panels, a scrollbar may appear in one or more of the panels.

import video p. 4

- Encoder can import a variety of video formats, including, but not limited to, MOV, MP4, MPEG, and WMV. The Importing > Supported file formats section of the User Guide contains a complete list of both video and audio formats, as well as more details concerning them.

- You may load more than one video into Encoder. Each additional imported video appears at the bottom of the list in the Media Content panel.

- Numerous interface elements— buttons, icons, form fields, and more—have a corresponding tooltip that describes more about the element when you hover the mouse pointer over it.

play video p. 6

- You may experience trouble playing back certain videos. For more information, consult the Importing > Troubleshoot playback problems section of the user guide.

customize workspace p. 7

- The workspace zoom range is 50–150. The default value is 100.
- Encoder remembers your workspace settings so they will be the default whenever you open the application.
- Use the Window > Hide Panels option to hide everything except the Media Player panel. The player will expand to occupy the entire Encoder interface. Choose the same menu option again to turn off this feature.
- If you prefer a lighter interface, go to Tools > Options. Then, in the Options dialog box, select Workspace at left and then Expression light from the Theme select box. The interface will switch to the new theme as a preview, but you must click the OK button to enact the change. The default theme is Expression dark. Note that the theme does not change when you use the Reset Active Workspace feature.

2. edit and crop video

Now that you have a basic feel for Encoder, let's start working with some video. Beginning in this chapter and continuing in the next two, you will learn how to prepare your video in a variety of ways prior to encoding it.

In this chapter, you will learn to:

Edit video in the beginning, middle, and end.

Crop your video so only a portion of it is shown.

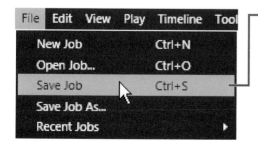

Save a job so you don't lose work.

If you don't have a video imported in Encoder already, follow the instructions in the Import Video section of Chapter 1 before proceeding.

edit video

In many cases, you may wish to encode an entire video, but Encoder also makes it easy for you to remove portions of it before encoding. For instance, you might have been adjusting the camera's focus at the beginning or someone may have walked in front of you a few minutes into shooting.

Keep in mind that when making edits in Encoder, your source video (the file you imported) will remain unchanged, so not to worry. The edits will only be made to the encoded version you will eventually output later in Chapter 5. In fact, even if you try to overwrite your source video when outputting the encoded one, Encoder won't let you.

In the steps that follow, we'll imagine you would like to remove a section from the beginning, end, and somewhere in between. The specific areas you would like to edit your video may be different than shown in this chapter, but the principles of editing remain the same.

Encoder keeps track of all video edits in the Clip Edits module.

1 In the tabbed panel, click the Enhance panel tab header to reveal the Clip Edits module.

Clip Edits lists the start and end times of our video by default.

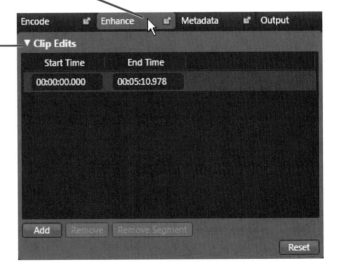

edit and crop video

Let's remove a section from the beginning of the video.

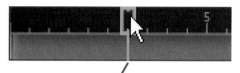

1 Drag the playhead to approximately the 00:00:03.000 (that is to say, 3 second) mark. You may find it helpful to keep your eye on the Position indicator as you do so to see how close you're getting. However, don't worry if you can't get too precise right now. You'll learn how to do that in just a bit.

(See extra bits on page 21.)

2 Right-click anywhere on the timeline, and select Mark In to remove the first 3 seconds from the video.
(See extra bits on page 21.)

Note that the Duration indicator has updated to reflect that your video is now about 3 seconds shorter.

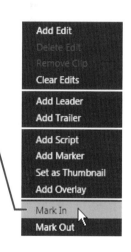

Similarly, the Clip Edits module has updated to reflect that our video's Start Time has changed. (See extra bits on page 21.)

Start Time	End Time
00:00:03.015	00:05:10.978

edit video (cont.)

Removing a section from the end of the video is nearly the same process. This time, though, let's choose a more precise point from which to begin our edit.

1 Drag the zoom slider all the way to the right. Alternatively, you could click the Zoom in icon.

Zoom slider

Zoom out — Zoom in

2 Drag the playhead to approximately the 00:00:11.376 mark. (See extra bits on page 21.)

3 Right-click anywhere on the timeline, and select Mark Out to remove everything after the mark.

Once again, Clip Edits has been updated, this time to reflect our new End Time.

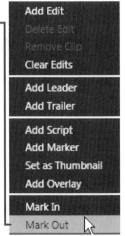

Start Time	End Time
00:00:03.015	00:00:14.391

Finally, let's remove a selection elsewhere in the video.

1 Drag the playhead to approximately the 00:00:04.487 mark.

2 Click the Add Edit button below the timeline to mark this as the starting point of our edit. (See extra bits on page 21.)

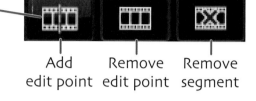

Add edit point   Remove edit point   Remove segment

3 Drag the playhead to approximately the 00:00:05.401 mark.

4 Click the Add Edit button again to mark this as the ending point of our edit.

The timeline now has two vertical bars marking our edit points, and the Clip Edits module lists them as well.

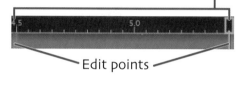

Edit points

Start Time	End Time
00:00:03.015	00:00:07.502
00:00:07.502	00:00:08.416
00:00:08.416	00:00:14.391

First edit point

Second edit point

5 Click the ◄|◄ button to move the playhead back to the first edit point. (See extra bits on page 21.)

6 Click the ▷X◁ button to remove the video segment between the two edit points. Your video duration is now approximately 00:00:10.462.

Note that the start point of our edit was removed along with the video segment, so the timeline now only has the second vertical edit bar we added.

crop video

Unlike editing, cropping does not change the duration of video, only what portion of its full width and height is viewable. For instance, you might have visual noise at the edges or activity that isn't relevant to the focus of your video. Cropping allows you to remove those elements from the encoded version.

1 Click the `Encode` ⊡ panel tab header.

2 In the Video Profile module, click the Crop checkbox to enable the crop mode. (See extra bits on page 22.) Depending on your screen resolution, you may need to scroll down to see the Crop section.

Position of crop from left edge of video

Position of crop from top edge of video

Width of cropped area

Height of cropped area

Reset crop to default

3 The red box around the video indicates you are in Crop mode. Hover over the bottom-right square handle until the pointer changes to a diagonal double-arrow. Drag the corner up and over until the width is about thirty pixels narrower. (Note: The Width and Height values in the Video Profile module's Crop section change as you drag the handle). (See extra bits on page 22.)

edit and crop video

4 Hover over the red outline (but not over a handle) until the pointer changes to four arrows. Drag the Crop box five pixels down and fifteen pixels to the right. (Note: The Left and Top values in the Video Profile module's Crop section change as you drag the box.)

Your final crop settings are reflected in the Video Profile module's Crop section. Your video's Width and Height values may vary.

save job

Just as you periodically save your work when working with a word processor or spreadsheet, it's a good idea to save your progress—called a job—in Encoder so you won't lose your work in the event your computer has problems or you exit the application.

When you save a job, a record is kept of video-related work but not any adjustments you've made to the workspace or theme.

1 Choose Save Job from the File menu.

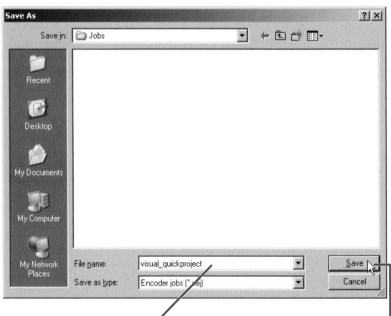

2 Since this is our first time saving the job, the Save As dialog box appears. Enter visual_quickproject as the file name, and click Save. (See extra bits on page 22.)

extra bits

edit video p. 14

- Note that the amount of space between "teeth" in your timeline may be different than what is shown. Encoder adjusts the default view of the timeline based on the length of the imported video.

- If you do not see the time on the timeline to which you are trying to move the playhead, drag the playhead all the way to the edge. The timeline will scroll. Similarly, you could use the scrollbar directly below the timeline to shift the timeline left and right.

- You may click an edit in the Clip Edits module to jump to its start point on the timeline.

- You can undo an edit either by selecting it in the Clip Edits module and clicking the Remove button or by moving the playhead to an edit marker on the timeline and clicking the Remove Edit button. You can remove all edits with the Reset button in the Clip Edits module. The same action can be performed by right-clicking the timeline and choosing Clear Edits.

- You can manually enter a point at which you would like to edit video instead of dragging the playhead to it. Do so by clicking the time under the Position indicator and typing in the time.

- The start and end times shown in the Clip Edits module are relative to the entire length of your video before you made any edits. This may be confusing initially since when you make an edit, the timeline does change to reflect the adjusted duration. If you would like to see the original state of the video prior to making any edits, click the ▮▮▮ button below the timeline to show the cut regions. Each edited region will show as red in the timeline. You can play the entire video while in this mode as if you hadn't made any edits. Click the same button again to hide the edited regions.

- You may change your edits manually in the Clip Edits module by clicking on either the start or end time for a particular edit and typing in the time you would like.

extra bits (cont.)

crop video p. 18

- The video zoom menu (100% ▾) allows you to alter the video view in the Media Player panel. This can be useful if, for example, you are cropping a video and would like to zoom in to get a closer look at where you are setting the cropping borders. The zoom tool does not affect the size of the video itself, however.

- Turn off Crop mode by clicking the Crop checkbox so the check mark no longer appears. This will not erase your crop settings, but they won't be applied to your video unless the checkbox is checked.

- When the Maintain Aspect Ratio checkbox is checked, the ratio of the width and height of the cropped area will remain consistent with the uncropped video as you resize it.

- Drag a handle on the side to adjust the width of the crop box. Drag a corner handle to adjust the width and height simultaneously.

- As an alternative to dragging a crop box handle, you can define the Left, Top, Width and Height values of the crop box manually in the Crop module. Simply click one of the values to select it and type a new one.

- The Reset button will restore the default crop settings for Left, Top, Width and Height.

- Consult Modify video > To set video aspect ratios in the User Guide for more information about aspect ratios.

save job p. 20

- It is important to leave each asset where it was on your hard drive at the time of saving a job. Otherwise, Encoder will not be able to locate them when you open the job.

edit and crop video

3. add a leader, trailer, and overlay

Now that you've edited and cropped your video, it's time to enhance it further. In this chapter, you will learn to:

Add a leader before your video.

Credits

Eagle: The Eagle
Camera Operator: Me

Add a trailer after your video.

Add an overlay to your video.

Resize and reposition your overlay.

Encoder provides tools to add optional content both before and after your video in the form of a leader and trailer, respectively. This allows you to include, for example, an opening sequence and closing credits, or pre- and post-roll ads. Furthermore, you may overlay content, such as a watermark, on top of your video.

Encoder combines all of these assets into one outputted video when you perform the encode operation, as you will see later in the book.

The silverlightvqj.zip file you downloaded from the companion Web site contains the leader.png, trailer.png, and overlay.png files we will use in this chapter.

open job

Open your saved job before proceeding if you closed it after the previous chapter.

1 Select File > Open Job.

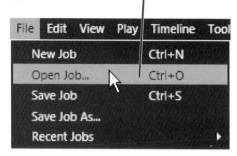

2 In the Open dialog box, select the job file and click Open.

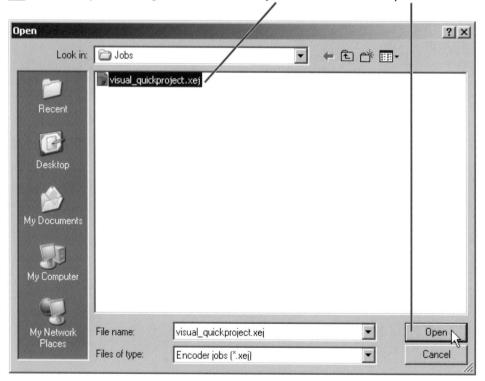

add a leader, trailer, and overlay

add a leader and trailer

First, let's add the leader:

1 Click the [Enhance] panel tab header.

2 Click the Add Leader checkbox in the Auto Stitch module. (You may need to scroll down to see the module.) The Add Leader file dialog box will appear.

3 In the Add Leader dialog box, navigate to the location where you placed the visual_quickproject/assets folder. In the images subfolder, select leader.png and click Open.

add a leader and trailer (cont.)

4 Click the Image Duration box and change the value from 00:00:01.000 to 00:00:02.500. This specifies how long the leader image will display before the video begins. (See extra bits on page 31.)

Image Duration 00:00:02.500

The leader is indicated at the beginning of the timeline by a green bar. ──── (See extra bits on page 31.)

To add a trailer, click the Add Trailer checkbox and repeat steps 3 and 4 above, using trailer.png as your trailer image and setting its duration to 00:00:03.000. The trailer will also appear on the timeline as a green bar, but at the end. (See extra bits on page 31.)

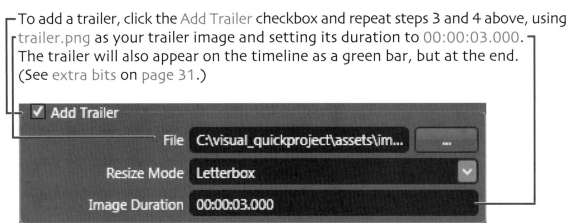

✓ Add Trailer

File C:\visual_quickproject\assets\im... ...

Resize Mode Letterbox

Image Duration 00:00:03.000

Let's play back the video to see how our leader and trailer look. If the playhead isn't at the beginning of the timeline, drag it or click the ◄ until it's at position 00:00:00.000, and press play to see your handiwork.

add an overlay

Now we're ready to add an overlay to the video. (See extra bits on page 32.)

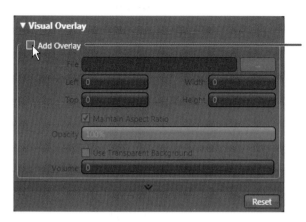

1 In the Enhance panel, click the Add Overlay checkbox in the Visual Overlay module.

2 In the Select the file to use as a video overlay dialog box, navigate to the location where you placed the visual_quickproject/assets folder. In the images subfolder, select overlay.png and click Open.

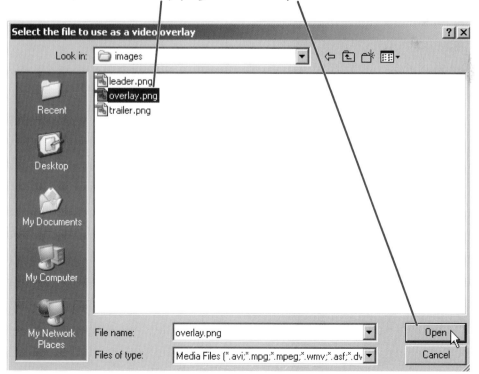

add a leader, trailer, and overlay

add an overlay (cont.)

3 By default, an overlay only appears over the main video, not the leader or trailer. So, depending where you are in the timeline at the moment, you may not see it. Drag the playhead to the 00:00:02.500 position, the point just after the leader where the video begins.

Overlay

Overlay duration

We do want our overlay to appear over the leader and trailer, however, so we'll adjust a setting for that. We'll also fade it in and out.

1 Toward the bottom above the Visual Overlay module, click the down arrow to expand the module and reveal more options.

2 In the Duration section that now appears, select Whole Sequence from the Apply to dropdown.

3 In the Fade Duration section, click the time next to Fade In and enter 00:00:01.000 so the overlay will take one second to fade in. (See extra bits on page 32.)

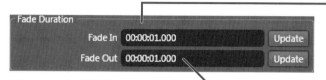

4 Click the time next to Fade Out and enter 00:00:01.000 so the overlay will take one second to fade out.

Our overlay is a little too large, so let's resize it. The current width and height are shown in the Visual Overlay module. You can manually enter new values there or resize the overlay as follows:

1 Grab the corner handle of the green box outlining the overlay and drag it until the width and height is 80x60. (See extra bits on page 32.)

Now let's move the overlay to the other bottom corner. Its position is dictated by how many pixels it is from the left and top sides of our video window, as shown in the Overlay module.

add a leader, trailer, and overlay

add an overlay (cont.)

1 Hover anywhere over the overlay (except a handle) until you see the icon with four arrows, and then click and drag the overlay to the left. (See extra bits on page 32.)

Finally, we'll adjust the overlay's opacity so it doesn't draw too much attention away from the video itself.

1 Click the value in the Opacity box, type 40, and hit Enter. (See extra bits on page 32.)

Opacity 40

Play everything back again from the beginning to see your overlay fade in 1 second into the leader, followed by the video, and then followed by the overlay fading out in the final second of the trailer.

Don't forget to save your job before continuing.

add a leader, trailer, and overlay

extra bits

add a leader and trailer p. 25

- The leader and trailer can be a video, image, audio, or XAML file. (XAML is the markup language used by Silverlight to define interface layouts, transformations, and animations.) More information is available in the User Guide under Modify video > Add leaders and trailers.

- If you choose a video as a leader or trailer, you cannot specify its duration like you can for an image since its duration will be the length of the video itself.

- You cannot edit a leader or trailer video in Encoder. You may, however, import a video you intend to use as a leader

or trailer, edit it as shown in Chapter 2, encode it as shown in Chapter 5, and then choose it as a leader or trailer.

- You can remove the leader by unchecking the Add Leader checkbox or right-clicking the timeline and selecting Remove Leader from the menu.

- You can remove the trailer by unchecking the Add Trailer checkbox or right-clicking the timeline and selecting Remove Trailer from the menu.

- You can clear both the leader and trailer entries in the Auto Stitch module with the Reset button at the bottom.

add a leader, trailer, and overlay   **31**

extra bits (cont.)

add an overlay p. 27

- A Visual Overlay can be an image, video, or XAML file. You can also add an Audio Overlay, such as for a voiceover track. More information about both overlay types is available in the User Guide under Encode your video for Microsoft Silverlight and the web > Overlays.

- You can create a custom duration for an overlay so it only appears during a portion of playback. In the Duraton module, select Custom from the Apply to drop-down, and the specify the Start and End times.

- The Fade In and Fade Out times represent how long it takes for the fades to occur, not the point on the timeline at which you would like the fading to take place. However, if, for example, you wanted the fade out to begin at the 9 second mark, you may drag the playhead to that point on the timeline and then click the Update button next to the Fade Out time. Encoder will calculate the fade out duration for you.

- You can change the Width and Height manually by clicking one of the values and typing the new value in the box.

- By default, the overlay resizes proportionally because the Maintain Aspect Ratio checkbox is checked. Uncheck it if you would like to change either the width or height independently of the other.

- You can change the Top and Left positions manually by clicking one of the values and typing the new position in the box.

- The opacity can also be adjusted by dragging the Opacity bar horizontally. The opacity of the overlay will adjust as you do this, allowing you to see the setting you prefer.

- You can clear all overlay settings with the Reset button at the bottom of the Overlay module.

- Uncheck the Add Overlay box if you wish to remove the overlay (some settings will remain intact in case you wish to add the overlay back again).

add a leader, trailer, and overlay

4. metadata, markers, and captions

In this chapter we will prepare our video for encoding further. Specifically, we will:

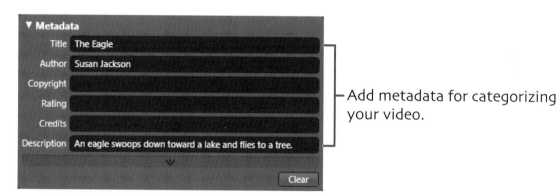 Add metadata for categorizing your video.

 Add markers to enable DVD-style chaptering in your outputted video player.

Add a caption to show at a specific point of your encoded video.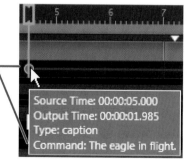

Open your saved job (see Chapter 3) before proceeding if you closed it after finishing the previous chapter.

add metadata

Metadata is information about your video that does not appear in the video itself. It is helpful for categorizing your video so that it may be organized and located more easily. For instance, imagine you have hundreds of videos and you use a digital-asset-management (DAM) tool to catalog them. (See extra bits on page 39.)

Let's add some metadata to your video.

1 Click the [Metadata] tab header.

2 Click the Title field, and type a title for your video.

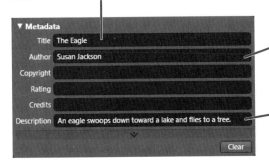

3 Hit TAB to advance to the Author field, and type the name of your video's author.

4 Hit TAB until you advance to the Description field, and type your video's description.

The Metadata module only shows a handful of metadata fields by default, but Encoder has dozens more you can use. Click the ⌄ to expand the module and reveal the additional metadata fields.

Now let's add a custom field to the bottom of this list.

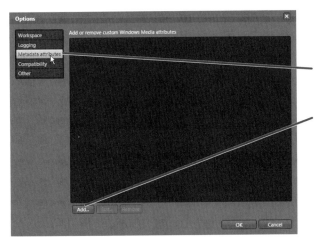

1 Select Tools > Options from the main menu.

2 Click the Metadata attributes button in the Options dialog box.

3 Click the Add button. A small dialog box will appear on top of the Options dialog box.

metadata, markers, and captions

4 Type the name of the custom metadata attribute you would like to create in the "Name of Windows Media attribute" field and click OK.

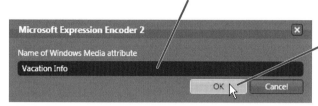

5 The new field now appears in the list of custom Metadata attributes. (See extra bits on page 39.) Click OK to close the Options dialog box.

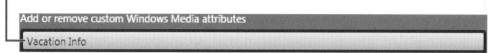

Now that we have created a custom field, we can associate a value with it for our video.

1 If necessary, scroll to the bottom of the Metadata module. Type your metadata in the field you just created ("Vacation Info" in our example). (See extra bits on page 39.)

Scroll bar

metadata, markers, and captions   **35**

add markers

A marker is a point you specify in the timeline, like putting a stake in the ground on a trail. (See extra bits on page 39.) One common use for markers in Encoder is to create DVD-style chapters in your outputted Silverlight video player, allowing the viewer to jump to points within your video. A marker cannot be placed on either the leader or trailer.

We'll create the markers here in preparation for outputting the player in Chapter 6.

1 Drag the playhead to approximately the 00:00:07.220 ————— position of the timeline.

2 Click the Add button in the Markers module of the Metadata panel. The marker is now listed in the module. (See extra bits on page 39.)

▼ **Markers**

Time	Value	☐ Thum	☑ Key F
00:00:08.649	[iown Value]	☐	☑

Add	Remove	Edit	Update Time

Import	Export	Clear

Value

Chapter 1

3 Click the Value field and type Chapter 1 to name the marker (any name is fine). (See extra bits on page 39.)

4 Click the Thumbnail checkbox.
The thumbnail will show in the video
player you will output later, indicating the
chapter point to which the viewer can jump.

5 Click the ⌄ at the bottom of the Markers module to reveal the advanced
properties.

6 In the Size module, click the Width field and type 150 to set the width of
our marker thumbnail. The Height value will change proportionally because the
Maintain Aspect Ratio checkbox is selected by default.

The marker is shown not only as an item in the Markers module list but also as a
white arrow on the timeline. (See extra bits on page 39.) If you hover over the
arrow, you will see both the marker's Time and Value.

Repeat steps 2 to 4 above to put a second chapter marker at the 00:00:10.500
position, using Chapter 2 as the value.

add captions

A caption is text that displays over the video at a timeline position that you define. The most obvious uses for this are to provide closed captioning that mirrors your video's dialogue or subtitles in another language. Another application could be to provide running commentary about the video. (See extra bits on page 40.) Each caption is defined with a Script Command, which as you'll see, is not all that different than a marker in terms of how it is created.

1 Drag the playhead to the 00:00:05.000 position.

2 Click the Add button in the Script Commands module of the Metadata panel (you might need to scroll down to see the module). The partially defined Script Command is now listed in the module.

3 Select caption from the Type dropdown menu.

4 Click the Command field and type the caption text you would like to appear in the video.

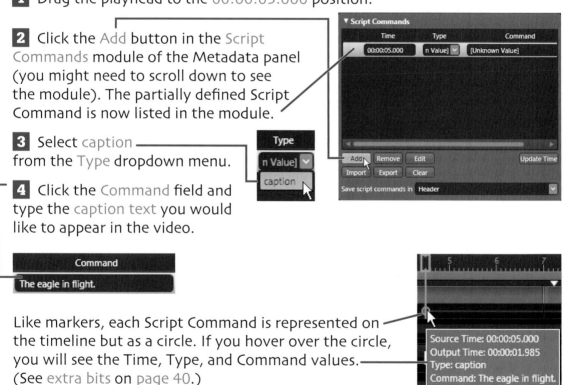

Like markers, each Script Command is represented on the timeline but as a circle. If you hover over the circle, you will see the Time, Type, and Command values. (See extra bits on page 40.)

Repeat the steps above if you would like to add more captions.

As always, save your job before continuing.

metadata, markers, and captions

extra bits

add metadata p. 34

- More information about metadata is available in the User Guide under Modify video > Add metadata.
- The Clear button resets the metadata fields so they are blank.
- You can add more custom fields by following the same process.
- To edit a custom field, select it from the list in the Metadata attributes window of the Options dialog box and click the Edit button. Do the same but with the Remove button to delete a custom field.
- Each custom field appears at the bottom of the Metadata module in the order in which you create it.

add markers p. 36

- More information about markers is available in the User Guide under Modify video > Add script commands.
- You can add as many as 1,000 markers to a video.
- Note that the Time listed for a marker in the Markers module is different than the position to which you dragged the playhead when setting the marker. This is because the timeline position includes the duration of the leader, whereas the marker Time reflects the point on only the video (since a marker cannot be put on a leader).

- To remove a marker, click on it in the Markers module and click the Remove button.
- The Export button exports your markers as an XML file. Conversely, the Import button imports a markers XML file. The combination of these features allows you to apply the same markers to other videos without having to add the markers in the manner demonstrated in this chapter. Additionally, if you are comfortable with XML, you could write a markers file manually and import it into Encoder.
- You can type whatever you would like in the Value field, as it is merely a way for you to identify a particular marker. As such, it does not need to include a chapter number in order for the DVD-style chaptering to work.
- You can change a marker's time in a few ways. One is to drag the marker arrow on the timeline. Another is if you drag the playhead but not the marker, the Update Time button in the Markers module will move the highlighted marker to that point. And, of course, you can also adjust the time manually by clicking on the Time field and typing in a new position. You may edit the Value field in a similar manual fashion.

add captions p. 38

- Script Commands can be used for other purposes besides displaying captions. More information about Script Commands is available in the User Guide under Modify video > Add script commands.

- The Clear button removes all Script Commands.

- Captions are only visible after outputting an encoded video (shown later in the book), not when playing back a video in Encoder.

5. encode video

Encoding is the process of taking your source video and outputting it according to settings that determine its format, quality and file size. As we've seen, Encoder allows one to input several video formats. Its output format for use with Silverlight 2 is VC-1 (H.264 support is on the way), which can be used in a variety of venues besides the Web.

In this chapter, we will:

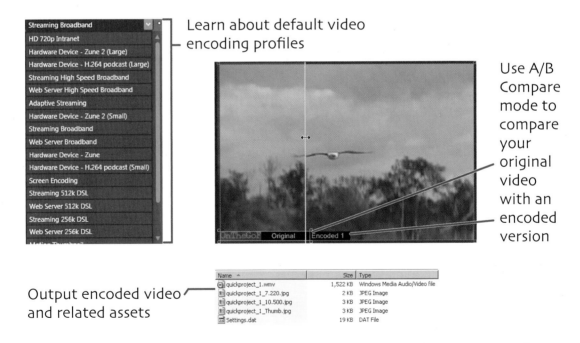

Learn about default video encoding profiles

Use A/B Compare mode to compare your original video with an encoded version

Output encoded video and related assets

Create and save a custom profile

Open your saved job before proceeding if you closed it after the previous chapter.

choose a profile

An Encoder profile is a collection of settings (affecting video and audio quality and more) used for encoding. There are two primary benefits to using a profile: You save time by not having to select the individual settings each time you want to encode a video, and you ensure consistency when encoding more than one video.

As we'll see in just a bit, you can define a custom profile. However, what's nice is Encoder has saved you a lot of trouble and head-scratching by providing several preconfigured default profiles that match common target encoding scenarios, particularly (but not exclusively) for the Web. Let's take a look at how to apply one of these.

1 Make sure you are in the Encode panel, and then from the Profile module, select Web Server Broadband from the Video menu. (See extra bits on page 54.)

Video profile

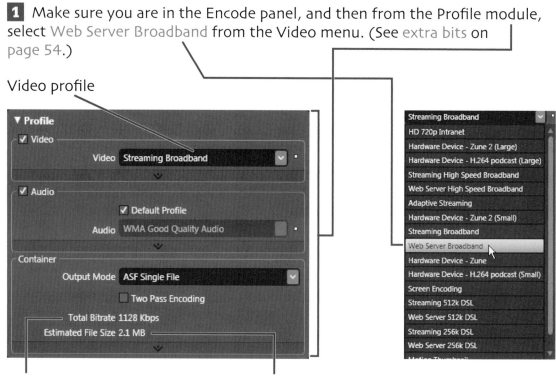

Total bitrate with this profile (value for your video will likely be different than what is shown).

Estimated file size of video when encoded with this profile (value for your video will likely be different than what is shown).

encode video

In this case, the Total Bitrate and Estimated File Size indicators in the Container section likely did not change for you because the profile you selected was the same broadband setting except for changing the server type from Streaming to Web Server. Had you chosen a profile such as Web Server 512k DSL, however, these values would have gone down in support of targeting users with a less robust Internet connection. The video dimensions are also affected by the profile selected.

Now that you have chosen a profile, you could output your encoded video (without an accompanying Silverlight video player) at this point by simply clicking the Encode button. No other work would be required. However, we want to explore other options before encoding and outputting our video.

use a/b compare mode

A/B Compare is one of Encoder's most helpful features because it enables you to find the right mix of video and audio quality in relation to file size. (See extra bits on page 54.) When in A/B Compare mode, you can watch a section of your video that has two different settings next to each other. You can use it to compare the source video quality next to one encoding setting or compare the quality of two different encoding settings.

From a quality standpoint, this allows you to find the settings that suit your video much more quickly than outputting an encoded video, watching it, and then going back into Encoder to adjust encoding settings until you get them optimized. Plus, you can see the estimated file size without waiting to encode the video.

Let's see how it works:

1 Drag the playhead to the approximate point of the video that you would like to compare. It is best to compare a more complicated or busier section of the video.

2 Click the A/B compare button at the bottom of the Media Content panel to enter the mode. (The button toggles to Exit A/B compare once you're in the mode.)

The "A" version of the video that appears in left half of Media Panel for comparison.

The "B" version of the video that appears in right half of Media Panel for comparison once Build Preview is clicked.

Compare Mode menu defaulted to Split.

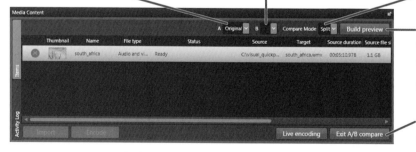

Builds a preview of your video using the video profile you selected.

Exit A/B compare mode.

3 There are a few comparison modes from which to choose (see extra bits on page 54), but Encoder defaults to Split, as reflected in both the Compare Mode drop-down menu and the Media Panel. The left half shows your video in its Original (unencoded) state, and the right half, currently black, will eventually show (a couple steps from now) that side of the video encoded per the profile you selected. Drag the vertical bar in the middle to show more or less of the Original video side. (See extra bits on page 54.)

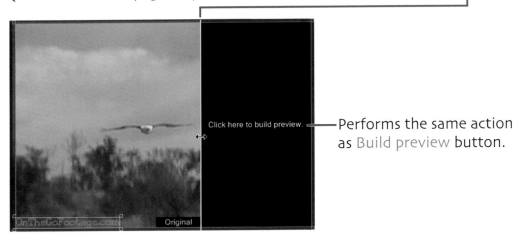

Click here to build preview. ——Performs the same action as Build preview button.

Original

4 The white square bracket on each side of the playhead indicates the section of video that will be compared. By default, Encoder puts the open bracket 3 seconds before where you placed the playhead and the close bracket 3 seconds after it. Drag either of the brackets to adjust the section. (Note that you can hit the play button and the currently bracketed section will play in a loop to help you judge if this is the portion you would like to compare.)

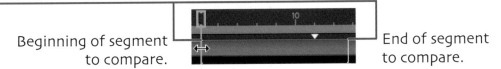

Beginning of segment to compare.

End of segment to compare.

5 Click either the Build preview button or the black area of the Split view (see image in Steps 2 and 3). Encoder will then encode the section of video. The time it takes to do so will vary and is indicated in the Status column of the Media Content panel. (See extra bits on page 54.)

Status

Pass 1 of 2: 00:00:40

use a/b compare mode (cont.)

When the preview is ready, the video will reappear in the media panel in a paused state. Additionally, the encoded version now appears as an option in both the A and B comparison drop-down menus.

The original video as "A" version.

The encoded video as "B" version.

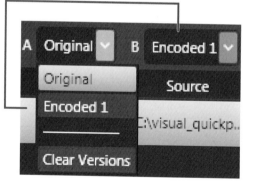

With the video paused, you can begin to see the differences between the Original video and the encoded version, though they would be more obvious had you chosen a lesser video profile such as Web Server 256k DSL or Web Server 512k DSL. (See extra bits on page 55.)

Once you click the Play button, the video will loop through the selected area, allowing you to see more of the differences. You can drag the yellow separator line to adjust the size of the split regions in either pause or play modes.

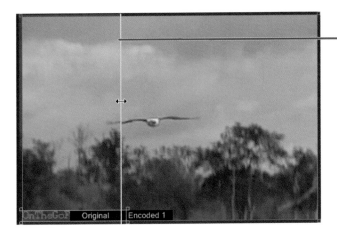

You have just seen how to compare the original video with a version encoded per a video profile. You can just as easily compare different profiles, whether they are among those preconfigured in Encoder or a custom one you create. This allows you to really home in on the settings that result in the best video for your needs.

Next, we'll look at how to create, test, and save a custom profile.

create custom profile

You can create a custom profile by modifying any of the settings assigned to a default profile in either the Profile or Advanced Codec Settings modules. (See extra bits on page 55.)

Why might you want to customize a profile? Well, let's imagine you are a little concerned about your video's file size using the Web Server Broadband profile but you don't want to compromise its quality and dimensions too much by going down to the Web Server 512k DSL profile.

Let's create a custom profile based on Web Server Broadband, which you can then test with A/B Compare.

1 If you have selected a different profile since earlier in the chapter, select Web Server Broadband from the Video profile drop-down menu.

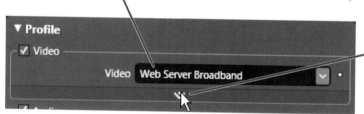

2 Click the down arrow at the bottom of the Video section of the Profile module to reveal the advanced properties.

3 Hover over the Bitrate(average) box so the pointer with four arrows appears. Then drag left until the value goes down to 850. Alternatively, as with like boxes, you could click on the box, type 850 and hit Enter.

Custom Bitrate(average) setting

Resulting Total Bitrate and Estimated File Size

Custom profile default name

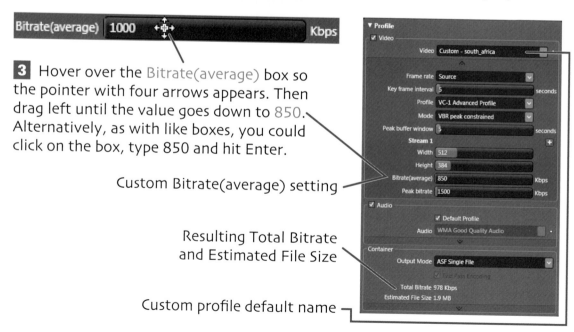

That single change triggers a few updates in the Profile module. First, as expected, the Total Bitrate and Estimated File Size values have gone down because you have decreased the video quality due to a lower bitrate average. However, Encoder has also changed your profile selection from Web Server Broadband to Custom followed by a hyphen and your video name. This is the default name given to your custom profile.

If you did not exit A/B compare mode after your first test, then as a result of the change to the Bitrate(average) value, Encoder has replaced the B side of the video with a prompt to build a new preview. (If you did exit it, click the A/B compare button before continuing.)

Let's build a preview using your custom profile and compare it to the Web Server Broadband profile we tested initially.

1 As before, click either the Build preview button or the black area to build a preview of your video using your custom setting.

The new preview is indicated as Encoded 2 in both the video window and the B menu. (See extra bits on page 55.)

create custom profile (cont.)

2 Select Encoded 1 from the A menu to compare your first profile test (Web Server Broadband) with your second (Custom).

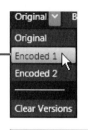

Notice that Encoder did not need to rebuild the preview for Web Server Broadband since it had stored it in memory as Encoded 1.

Play through the loop as before to compare the two profiles. Click the Exit A/B compare button when you are finished.

Assuming you preferred the custom profile, let's save it in case you would like to use it on other videos in the future.

1 Click the small white box to the right of the Video profile drop-down menu and select Save.

2 In the Save Profiles dialog box that appears, type the name you would like to use to define your custom profile and click OK.

Your saved custom profile now appears in the Video profile menu.

output video

You are finally ready to output your video for use on the Web and elsewhere. For now, you will only be outputting your video, not a Silverlight player template along with it (that will come shortly). It's important to know how to output a video on its own considering you are more likely to perform that task regularly, whereas you may only need to output a player once to support your videos.

Let's begin:

1 Make sure you have selected the Video profile you would like to use.

2 Click the Output panel tab header to reveal the panel.

3 Click Best Frame in the Thumbnail module to allow Encoder to decide which still image to output with the video file (we will use the thumbnail later). (See extra bits on page 56.)

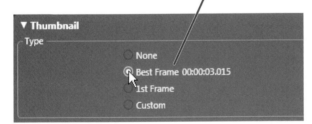

4 In the Size section of the Thumbnail module, click the Width box and type 100. The Height will adjust proportionally.

output video (cont.)

5 In the Job Output module, click the Media File Name box and replace {Original file name} with quickproject_1. Be careful to not remove the period (".") or {Default extension} that follows it. (See extra bits on page 56.)

6 Click the "..." button next to the Directory path box to select where to save the file.

7 In the Browse For Folder dialog box, navigate to the location where you created the visual_quickproject/site folder earlier, and then click OK.

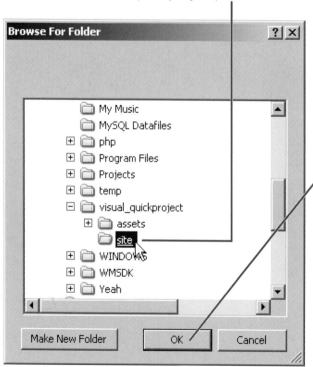

encode video

The Directory path now appears in the box.

8 Check the Sub-folder by Job ID checkbox to turn off that option.

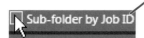

9 And finally, click the Encode button to both encode and output your video to the specified directory. (See extra bits on page 56.) The time it will take to encode will vary. The Status column displays the progress just as does when using A/B Compare.

Navigate to your directory once the encoding is finished to see the files Encoder outputted.

Encoded video

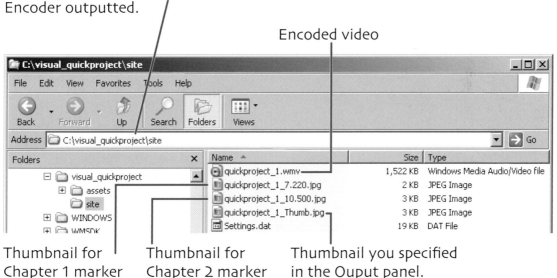

Thumbnail for   Thumbnail for   Thumbnail you specified
Chapter 1 marker   Chapter 2 marker   in the Ouput panel.

As always, save your job before continuing.

encode video

extra bits

choose a profile p. 42

- More information about profiles in general and default profiles in particular is available in the User Guide under Encode your video for Microsoft Silverlight and the web > Profiles and Define a default profile, respectively.

- In our example, we selected Web Server Broadband. Broken down, this means that this profile is targeted for a scenario in which the video lives on a Web server (which is likely to be the case for you rather than a streaming server), and the user who will watch the video has an Internet connection speed comparable to 1 Mbps or better. By comparison, the Web Server High Speed Broadband targets a 1.7 Mbps connection. Naturally, the quality of the video is better with these two and the file size is larger. Alternatively, the Web Server 512k DSL profile is fairly conservative, yielding a smaller video both in dimensions and file size, targeting a user with roughly half the speed as the Web Server Broadband profile.

a/b compare mode p. 44

- More information about A/B Compare is available in the User Guide under Encode your video for Microsoft Silverlight and the web > Compare encoding methods.

- There are four A/B Compare modes: Split, Bands, Side by Side, and Difference. These are available in the Compare Mode menu to the left of the Build preview button. Hover your mouse pointer over the menu to reveal the tooltip box that describes each of the modes. (Encoder fades the tooltip away after a few seconds, so you may need to hover more than once to read it all.). A couple additional notes are worth mentioning about the Bands mode. The first is that the bands alternate between the A and B views. Secondly, you can change the number of bands by dragging one of the yellow separators.

- In either Split or Bands modes, you can change the view from horizontal to vertical by double-clicking the yellow line (all of the lines do this in Bands).

- When you initiate the building of a preview, the Build preview button toggles to Cancel build, allowing you to stop the process if you click it.

- If you make a change to a video—like adding a marker—and encode it again, you'll notice that Encoder does it more quickly the second time. Encoder only encodes what has changed since the initial encoding, which can save a significant amount of time, particularly with a longer video.

- You may find it helpful to zoom into the video to see the differences between the A and B more clearly. You can change the zoom level percentage using the Zoom tool just above and to the left of the timeline. This only affects the view in the media panel and has no effect on the size of the video that you will output for use later in the chapter.

create a custom profile p. 48

- More information about Custom profiles is available in the User Guide under Encode your video for Microsoft Silverlight and the web > Custom profiles.

- The Default Profile checkbox in the Audio module dictates that the audio track will be encoded per the Video profile you selected. In our example, we are using the Web Server Broadband profile, which uses the WMA Good Quality Audio profile. You can choose a different Audio profile by unchecking the Default Profile checkbox and selecting a profile from the Audio dropdown menu. For instance, you might decide to use the WMA High Quality Audio profile to improve the audio track. As always, the Total Bitrate and Estimated File Size values in the Container module will indicate how your profile settings will impact the output-ted encoded video.

- Select Clear Versions from either the A or B menus to remove the encoding tests. Clicking the Exit A/B Compare clears them as well.

extra bits (cont.)

output video p. 51

- Not surprisingly, the 1st Frame option will use the video's first frame as the thumbnail image. The Custom option allows you to indicate a specific time in the video from which to generate the thumbnail.

- If you don't change the file name, Encoder names the outputted video file according to its original name. However, it will not write over the original.

- Practically speaking, you will likely prefer to name your videos in a manner that describes their content, such as cat_and_yarn.{Default extension} or boy_falls_off_bike.{Default extension}. We are using the quickproject_[number].{Default extension} convention here for the purpose of creating uniformity for all readers.

- After you click the Encode button, it toggles to Cancel encode. A Pause button also appears. Click that to temporarily halt the encoding.

6. output silverlight player

We're getting close! By the end of this chapter you will see your video played back in a Web page.

Along the way you will:

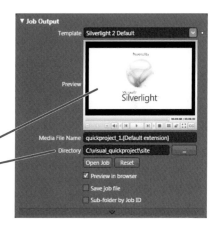

Choose a Silverlight 2 player template

Output your encoded video and video player

Preview it in a browser

Keep in mind that you won't have to output a player for each video you use on your site. Instead, you can reuse the player you will output in this chapter and follow the encoding process demonstrated in Chapter 5 to output videos without a player. If you are encoding multiple videos you expect to share some encoding parameters, you will want to understand how an Encoder Preset can save you time and how it differs from a Job or Profile. See extra bits on page 63 for more details.

Open your saved job before proceeding if you closed it after finishing the previous chapter.

choose player template

In Chapter 5, you learned how to output an encoded video on its own. Now, you will see how to output a Silverlight 2 video player with your video. (See extra bits on page 63–64.)

1 Click the Output tab header.

2 When you encoded a video in Chapter 5 without a player, you left the Template setting at (None). This time, select Silverlight 2 Default from the Template menu in the Job Output module. (See extra bits on page 63.)

If you have the Silverlight 2 plug-in installed then you will see a preview of the video player. (See extra bits on page 64.)

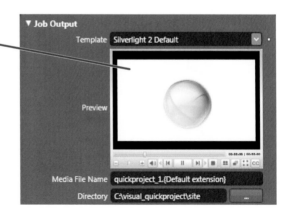

Media File Name | quickproject_1.{Default extension}
Directory | C:\visual_quickproject\site

3 Make sure to indicate the Media File Name and Directory as we did in Chapter 5. You can use the same file name for the video as before; Encoder won't re-create the video file if it sees it in the directory already.

4 Click the Encode button.

☑ Preview in browser

Because the Preview in browser option was selected by default, Encoder will open the player preview page in your default Web browser once it is finished encoding.

If you navigate to your visual_quickproject/site folder, you will notice that Encoder's output was the same as in Chapter 5 except for two new files: Default.html (the Web page that displays the video player) and MediaPlayerTemplate.xap (the Silverlight video player).

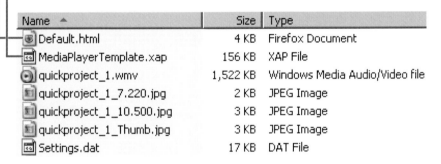

Name ▲	Size	Type
Default.html	4 KB	Firefox Document
MediaPlayerTemplate.xap	156 KB	XAP File
quickproject_1.wmv	1,522 KB	Windows Media Audio/Video file
quickproject_1_7.220.jpg	2 KB	JPEG Image
quickproject_1_10.500.jpg	3 KB	JPEG Image
quickproject_1_Thumb.jpg	3 KB	JPEG Image
Settings.dat	17 KB	DAT File

We will take a look at the player's features in the next section.

output silverlight player

preview in browser

By now, your player template has loaded in a Web page and your video is playing back automatically. (See extra bits on page 64.) The video should look as it did when you played it in Encoder with the exception that now the closed caption appears at the point where you set the Script Command in Chapter 4. (See extra bits on page 64.)

You may also have noticed that the video player was expanded to fill the entire page (if you resize your browser, the player will resize as well). This has less practical use, since typically you would like a video player to fit into a page with related content. We will be doing just that in forthcoming chapters, resizing the player to fixed dimensions as part of the effort.

Following is a summary of the video player's features:

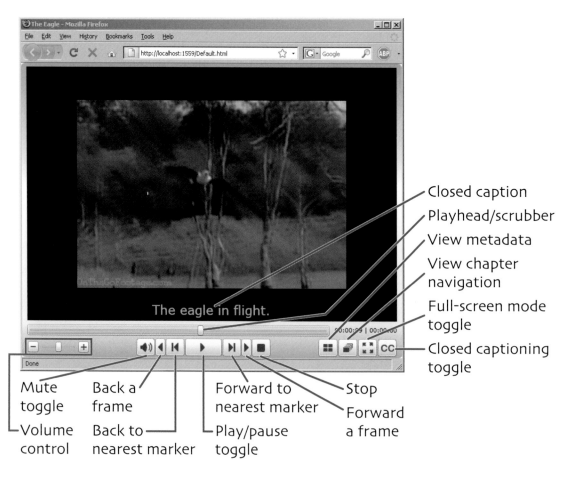

Closed caption
Playhead/scrubber
View metadata
View chapter navigation
Full-screen mode toggle
Closed captioning toggle

Mute toggle
Back a frame
Forward to nearest marker
Stop
Forward a frame
Volume control
Back to nearest marker
Play/pause toggle

Most of these features should be familiar to you, but let's explore a few of them in more depth, beginning with the metadata panel:

1 Click the metadata button to reveal the panel over the video.

The information shown are the Title and Description values you entered in the Metadata module in Chapter 4, and the image is the Best Frame 100 × 67 thumbnail (outputted as quickproject_1_Thumb.jpg) you defined in the Output panel in Chapter 5.

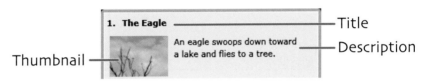

Thumbnail

Title

Description

2 Click the metadata button again to hide the panel.

Now, let's take a look at the chapter navigation panel:

1 Click the chapter navigation button to reveal the panel over the video.

The two chapters reflect the markers you defined in the Markers module in Chapter 4. The images are the 150 × 100 thumbnails defined in the same module and outputted as quickproject_1_7.220.jpg and quickproject_1_10.500.jpg (the file name suffixes will vary if you placed your markers at different times).

Thumbnails

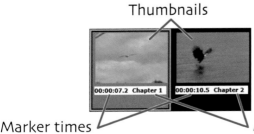

Marker times

Marker values

preview in browser (cont.)

2 Click a chapter to jump the video to that point.

00:00:10.5 Chapter 2

3 Click the chapter navigation button from step 1 again to hide the panel.

Finally, let's look at full-screen mode.

1 Click the full-screen button to switch the playback mode.

Your video now occupies the entire screen with no browser chrome. For the first few seconds, you will see a message saying, "Press ESC to exit full-screen mode."

Press ESC to exit full-screen mode.
http://localhost

2 Press (Esc) or click the full-screen button again to exit the mode.

output silverlight player

extra bits

introduction p. 57

- So far in this book, you have saved a Job and a Profile. To recap, a Job saves all settings you have made in the Encode, Enhance, Metadata, and Output panels as well as paths to the imported videos listed in the Media Content panel. A Profile, because it only pertains to encoding, saves only the settings in the Encode panel.

  We have not discussed Presets not previously, however. A Preset is much like a job in that it saves the Encode, Enhance, Metadata, and Output panel settings. However, it does not save the list of imported videos as a Job does. Additionally, a Preset only saves the panel settings relative to a specific video, whereas a Job may contain multiple videos with varying panel settings.

  You can probably see why using a Preset would be handy. Imagine you have ten videos you want to encode with the same overlay, metadata, encoding profile, and output settings. If saved as a Profile, these collective settings could be applied to all ten videos prior to encoding, saving you the time of going through the steps of creating them for each video. You can also apply more than one Preset to a video. More information about Presets is located in the User Guide at Encode your video for Microsoft Silverlight and the web > Create presets.

choose player template p. 58

- More information about outputting video with a player is available in the User Guide under Encode your video for Microsoft Silverlight and the web > Encode using Silverlight templates.

- Encoder has player templates for both Silverlight 1 and Silverlight 2. Since Silverlight 2 is the newer version, we will use one developed for that version. Your video will work with a Silverlight 1 player, however, the player files Encoder exports are different, so not all steps for the remainder of the book will match your needs.

extra bits (cont.)

choose player template (cont.)

- You need the Silverlight 2 plug-in installed both to view the player template preview in Encoder and to view your video player in a Web page. If you don't have it installed, you will see an install prompt in the preview area. Click it to begin the installation process (note: if you use Firefox and have it open, close it first.) Consult the System Requirements listed at http://www.microsoft.com/silverlight/resources/install.aspx#sysreq if you are experiencing any trouble.

preview in browser p. 60

- Encoder's default setting is to export a player that plays the video automatically in a Web page. This option as well as two others are accessible if you click the down arrow at the bottom of the Job Output module. If you uncheck the Automatically start video when cued option, the video will default to the first frame in pause mode instead of playing automatically. If you also uncheck Auto cue video when page is loaded, the Best Frame thumbnail (or whichever selected thumbnail type you chose) will show and the video won't load until the user initiates playback. This can result in a faster page load, but the user may need to wait a bit for the video to load.

- The final caption added to a video appears from the point on the timeline where its Script Command is set until the end of the video, including the trailer. Chances are your preference is to have the caption end sooner. If so, simply drag the playhead in Encoder to the point at which you would like it to end, and add a Script Command with a blank value in the Command field instead of caption text. Refer to the add captions section of Chapter 4 if you don't recall how to add a Script Command.

7. organize your files

Now that you have seen how to use Encoder to prepare and encode videos both with and without a player template, you will learn how to build our fictitious Web site, OnTheGoFootage, which incorporates your player and videos.

However, before jumping into the coding portion of building any site, it's always best to get a little organized.

In this chapter, you will learn to:

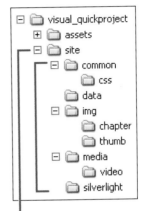

Create the site's folder structure

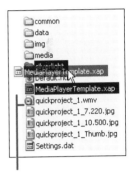

Move files into their proper folders

```
<object data="data:application/x-silverlight-2,"
type="application/x-silverlight-2" width="100%" height="100%">
    <param name="source" value="silverlight/MediaPlayerTemplate.xap"/>
    <param name="onerror" value="onSilverlightError" />
    <param name="initparams"
value='autoplay=True,autoload=True,enablecaptions=True,muted=False,stretchmode=
0,displaytimecode=False,playlist=<playList><playListItems><playListItem
title="The%20Eagle"
description="An%20eagle%20swoops%20down%20toward%20a%20lake%20and%20flies%20to%
20a%20tree." mediaSource="media/video/quickproject_1.wmv"
adaptiveStreaming="False" thumbSource="img/thumb/quickproject_1_Thumb.jpg"
frameRate="29.9676648895841" width="512" height="344" ><chapters><chapter
position="7.220" thumbnailSource="img/chapter/quickproject_1_7.220.jpg"
title="Chapter%201" /><chapter  position="10.500"
thumbnailSource="img/chapter/quickproject_1_10.500.jpg" title="Chapter%202"
/></chapters></playListItem></playListItems></playList>' />

    <a href="http://go2.microsoft.com/fwlink/?LinkID=124807"
style="text-decoration: none;">
        <img src="http://go2.microsoft.com/fwlink/?LinkId=108181" alt="Get
Microsoft Silverlight" style="border-style: none"/>
    </a>
</object>
```

Adjust the HTML code so it can locate each file in its new location

create folder structure

As we've seen, Encoder outputs all of its files to the same directory without any sense of hierarchy or organization.

Name ▲	Size	Type
Default.html	4 KB	Firefox Document
MediaPlayerTemplate.xap	156 KB	XAP File
quickproject_1.wmv	1,522 KB	Windows Media Audio/Video file
quickproject_1_7.220.jpg	2 KB	JPEG Image
quickproject_1_10.500.jpg	3 KB	JPEG Image
quickproject_1_Thumb.jpg	3 KB	JPEG Image
Settings.dat	17 KB	DAT File

Some might deem this acceptable for a small site, but we want to plan for one that is going to grow to perhaps include dozens of pages and videos some day. The site would be increasingly more difficult to manage if all the files were mixed together.

In the following steps, you will create folders to organize your images, video, Silverlight player, and other files that you will create in subsequent chapters:

1 Navigate to where you placed your visual_quickproject/site folder earlier.

2 While inside site, from Windows Explorer or Mac OS Finder, select File > New > Folder, and name the folder common. The common folder name is where we will store certain files shared by one or more pages in the site. (See extra bits on page 72.)

organize your files

3 Navigate inside the common folder, and create a folder within it named css. This folder will eventually contain the Cascading Style Sheets (CSS).

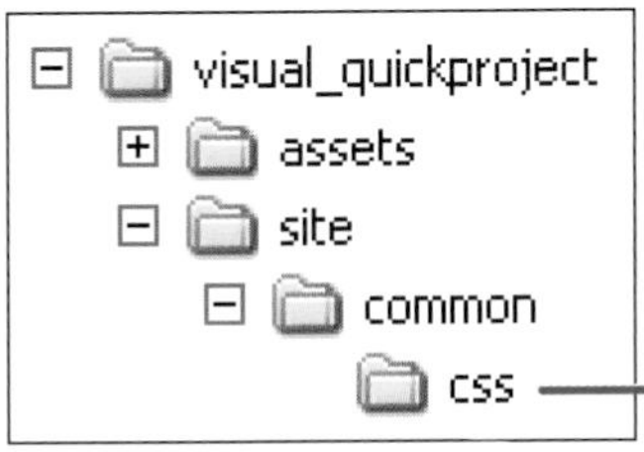

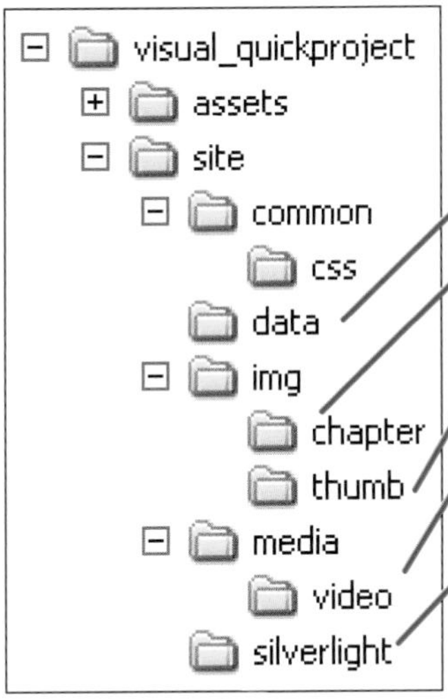

```
☐ 📁 visual_quickproject
   ⊞ 📁 assets
   ☐ 📁 site
      ☐ 📁 common
           📁 css ────────────────────────────┐
```

```
☐ 📁 visual_quickproject
   ⊞ 📁 assets
   ☐ 📁 site
      ☐ 📁 common
           📁 css
         📁 data
      ☐ 📁 img
           📁 chapter
           📁 thumb
      ☐ 📁 media
           📁 video
         📁 silverlight
```

4 Perform similar steps to create the following folders and subfolders:

- data
- img/chapter (in other words, a chapter folder inside an img folder)
- img/thumb
- media/video (this allows room for creating a media/audio folder later if you ever need one)
- silverlight

When you are finished, your folder structure should resemble the figure to the left.

move files into folders

Now that we have our structure in place, we can move the assets to the subfolders to which they belong.

1 Drag and drop MediaPlayerTemplate.xap from the site root to the silverlight subfolder.

2 Drag and drop the remaining files so they are moved into the correct subfolders listed below:

* quickproject_1.wmv to media/video
* quickproject_1_7.220.jpg to img/chapter
* quickproject_1_10.500.jpg to img/chapter
* quickproject_1_Thumb.jpg to img/thumb
* Settings.dat to data

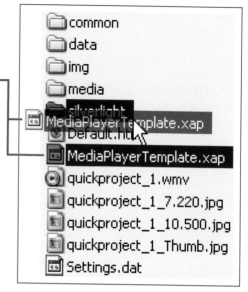

When you are done, Default.html should be the only file at the site root.

organize your files

update code

There is one final step we need to take before our reorganization is complete.

Default.html is the page that displays our video player. Because it uses the page assets we just moved, we need to adjust references to the assets in the code so the page will still work.

Copy and paste Default.html to make a backup of it before you get frustrated, just in case you make an error during the next set of steps and want to revert to a working version of the file.

Let's start updating the paths to the files:

1 Open Default.html in your text editor. (See extra bits on page 72.)

2 Scroll down until you see the `<object>`/`</object>` element. This code adds the Silverlight video player to the page and defines the location of assets and other information the player needs for playback.

```
<object data="data:application/x-silverlight-2,"
type="application/x-silverlight-2" width="100%" height="100%">
  <param name="source" value="MediaPlayerTemplate.xap"/>
  <param name="onerror" value="onSilverlightError" />
  <param name="initparams" value='autoplay=True,autoload=True,
enablecaptions=True,muted=False,stretchmode=0,
displaytimecode=False,playlist=<playList><playListItems>
<playListItem title="The%20Eagle" description="An%20eagle%20
swoops%20down%20toward%20a%20lake%20and%20flies%20to%20a%20tree."
mediaSource="quickproject_1.wmv" adaptiveStreaming="False"
thumbSource="quickproject_1_Thumb.jpg"
frameRate="29.9676648895841" width="512" height="344">
<chapters><chapter position="7.220"
thumbnailSource="quickproject_1_7.220.jpg" title="Chapter%201" />
<chapter position="10.500" thumbnailSource="quickproject_1_10.500.jpg"
title="Chapter%202" /></chapters></playListItem>
</playListItems></playList>' />
  <a href="http://go2.microsoft.com/fwlink/?LinkID=124807"
style="text-decoration: none;">
    <img src="http://go2.microsoft.com/fwlink/?LinkId=108181"
alt="Get Microsoft Silverlight" style="border-style: none"/>
  </a>
</object>
```

update code (cont.)

3 Change the path of the source param value from MediaPlayerTemplate.xap to silverlight/MediaPlayerTemplate.xap so the page will look for the Silverlight player in the silverlight subfolder.

```
<param name="source" value="silverlight/MediaPlayerTemplate.xap"/>
```

4 Change the mediaSource path to media/video/ quickproject_1.wmv so the page will look for the video in the media/video subfolder.

```
mediaSource="media/video/quickproject_1.wmv"
```

5 Change the thumbSource path to img/thumb/quickproject_1_Thumb.jpg so the page will look for the thumbnail in the img/thumb subfolder.

```
thumbSource="img/thumb/quickproject_1_Thumb.jpg"
```

6 Change the first thumbnailSource reference to img/chapter/quickproject_1_7.220.jpg and the second to img/chapter/quickproject_1_10.500.jpg so the page will look for the chapter navigation thumbnail images in img/chapter.

```
<chapters><chapter position="7.220" thumbnailSource=
"img/chapter/quickproject_1_7.220.jpg" title="Chapter%201" />
<chapter position="10.500" thumbnailSource="img/chapter/
quickproject_1_10.500.jpg" title="Chapter%202" /></chapters>
```

organize your files

When you are all done, your modified `<object>/</object>` element should resemble this:

```
<object data="data:application/x-silverlight-2,"
type="application/x-silverlight-2" width="100%" height="100%">
   <param name="source" value="silverlight/MediaPlayerTemplate.xap"/>
   <param name="onerror" value="onSilverlightError" />
   <param name="initparams" value='autoplay=True,autoload=True,
enablecaptions=True,muted=False,stretchmode=0,
displaytimecode=False,playlist=<playList><playListItems>
<playListItem title="The%20Eagle" description="An%20eagle%20
swoops%20down%20toward%20a%20lake%20and%20flies%20to%20a%20
tree." mediaSource="media/video/quickproject_1.wmv"
adaptiveStreaming="False" thumbSource="img/thumb/
quickproject_1_Thumb.jpg" frameRate="29.9676648895841"
width="512" height="344" ><chapters><chapter position="7.220"
thumbnailSource="img/chapter/quickproject_1_7.220.jpg"
title="Chapter%201" /><chapter position="10.500"
thumbnailSource="img/chapter/quickproject_1_10.500.jpg"
title="Chapter%202" /></chapters></playListItem>
</playListItems></playList>' />
   <a href="http://go2.microsoft.com/fwlink/?LinkID=124807"
style="text-decoration: none;">
     <img src="http://go2.microsoft.com/fwlink/?LinkId=108181"
alt="Get Microsoft Silverlight" style="border-style: none"/>
   </a>
</object>
```

7 Save Default.html so you can test the changes.

Now let's see if the page works with our updated paths.

1 Drag and drop Default.html into a browser to open the page and begin video playback.

Test the player's features, including the metadata and chapter navigation panels to be sure the thumbnail images show as expected.

extra bits

create folder structure p. 66

- The way "common" files are organized often varies from developer-to-developer, reflecting ones personal preference. You may have seen some sites use the folder name global instead of common, or simply have css and js (when a site requires JavaScript; ours does not) folders at the site root, rather than grouping them together in a parent folder. Any of these options is fine as long as the code pointing to a folder (as shown in this chapter) has the correct folder path and name.

update code p. 69

- A basic text editor is all that is required to write and edit code. For instance, if you are on a PC, Notepad will suffice. On the Mac, TextMate is a popular choice. However, do not use a word processor, as it may rewrite portions of the code you do not intend to change.

8. code site page

It's time to start creating our site. OnTheGoFootage is a fictional video site geared toward travel and adventure enthusiasts. Much like the popular video sites on the Web today, the content is both generated and submitted by users, documenting their adventures for others to experience secondhand.

The site will contain many conventions common to other video sites, namely a large video player, additional information related to the video that's playing, and links to play additional videos.

In this chapter, you will do the following as part of creating the site's main page:

add masthead

add fixed-sized video player

add more videos list

add video details

add footer

gather assets

There are a few more files you'll need to move into your site folders before you start to code the page.

Earlier, you downloaded the ZIP file from the companion Web site and extracted the files within it. It contains several images for the site.

1 Navigate to the visual_quickproject/assets/images/for_site_use folder.

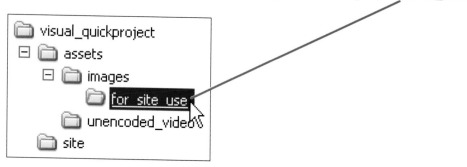

2 Copy and paste or move the following files from there to site/img:

- bg.gif
- bg_masthead.gif
- logo.gif

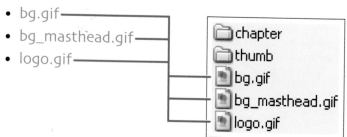

The bg_ files are background images and the logo, as you might expect, is the OnTheGoFootage logo.

3 Navigate back to the visual_quickproject/assets/images/for_site_use folder.

4 Copy and paste or move the following files from there to site/img/thumb:

- thumb_video_02.jpg
- thumb_video_03.jpg
- thumb_video_04.jpg
- thumb_video_05.jpg
- thumb_video_06.jpg
- thumb_video_07.jpg

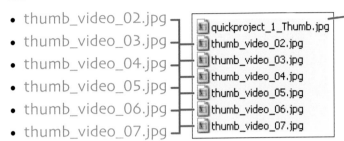

These are thumbnails representing imaginary videos we will be adding to our site. We have prefixed the file names with thumb_ to clearly differentiate them from any real thumbnails you may have outputted from Encoder, which end with _Thumb. (See extra bits on page 98.)

Now is a good time to gather any other videos you may have encoded, too. If you have additional videos you would like to test with the site, copy and paste them into site/media/video.

If you have companion thumbnails for them, move them into the folder shown in Step 4 above.

start html page

OK, with all assets in place, let's start coding. We'll begin with the skeleton of the HTML page. (Numbered captions refer to steps on page 77.)

Type the following code in your text editor of choice:

```
<!DOCTYPE html PUBLIC "-//W3C//DTD XHTML 1.0 Strict//EN"
  "http://www.w3.org/TR/xhtml1/DTD/xhtml1-strict.dtd">
<html xmlns="http://www.w3.org/1999/xhtml" xml:lang="en"
lang="en">
<head>
<title>On The Go Footage</title>                          1 Title
<meta http-equiv="Content-type" content="text/html;
charset=utf-8" />
<link rel="stylesheet" href="common/css/onthego.css"      2 Style
type="text/css" media="all" charset="utf-8" />              sheet

<!--[if lte IE 6]>
<link rel="stylesheet" href="common/css/onthego_ie6.css"
type="text/css" charset="utf-8" />
<![endif]-->
</head>
                                                          3 Small
                                                            style sheet
                                                            for IE6
<body>
<div id="container">
    <!-- Start Content -->
    <div id="content">
                                                          4 Main
                                                            container
    </div>
    <!-- end content -->
</div>
</body>
</html>
                                                          5 Content
                                                            container


6 HTML
  comments
```

1 Add the title that appears at the top-left of your browser (not within the Web page itself). (Steps refer to code on page 76.)

2 Load the style sheet you will create in the next section.

3 Load a small style sheet to provide rules specific to Internet Explorer 6.

4 Add the container that will house the code for the rest of your page.

5 Add the content container for your page.

6 HTML comments have no impact on your page's presentation. They are presented here as additional context for the code and to promote the practice of commenting your code to make it easier to read.

Most of the rest of the code above is required for setting the foundation for any HTML page and won't be visible to the user from a browser. It isn't important that you know all the ins-and-outs of what each portion does, just that you implement them correctly. (See extra bits on page 98.)

Save the file as index.html in the site directory.

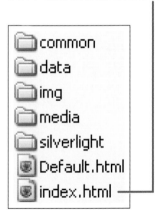

start style sheet

Now we'll apply some basic styling to the page via a Cascading Style Sheet (CSS). (See extra bits on page 98–99.) (Numbered captions refer to steps on page 80.)

Type the following code in your text editor of choice:

```
/* ------------------------------ */
/* ----- On the Go Footage ----- */
/* ------------------------------ */

/* Set Basics
------------------------------ */

/* Simplified Meyer Reset */
html, body, div, span, object, h1, h2, h3, h4, h5, h6,
p, a, img, ul, li, fieldset, form, label {
    margin: 0;
    padding: 0;
    border: 0;
    outline: 0;
    font-weight: inherit;
    font-style: inherit;
    font-size: 100%;
    font-family: inherit;
    vertical-align: baseline;
}

body {
    margin-bottom: 2em;
    font-family: arial, helvetica, sans-serif;
    line-height: 1;
    background: #dedad1 url(../../img/bg.gif) repeat-x 0 0;
}

body, input {
    color: #605e5c;
}
```

1 CSS comments

2 Simplified CSS reset method

3 Body styling

4 Baseline font color

```
ul {
  list-style: none;
}

h1, h2 {
  font-size: 1.315em;
  font-weight: bold;
  color: #242424;
}
```

5 Content header styles

```
/* Link colors */
a {
  text-decoration: none;
}

a:link, a:visited {
  color: #2d6600;
}

a:active, a:hover {
  color: #499c0d;
}

/* Page container
------------------------------ */
#container {
  width: 975px;
  margin: 0 auto;
}
```

6 Page width and centering

```
/* Content container
------------------------------ */
#content {
  overflow: auto;
}
```

code site page

start style sheet (cont.)

1 CSS comments have no impact on your page's presentation. They are presented here as additional context for the CSS and to promote the practice of both commenting and organizing your code. (Steps refer to code on page 78–79.)

2 Implement a simplified CSS Reset method. (See extra bits on page 98.)

3 Set styling to the body of our page, such as the font family and space between lines. This also defines our page background image and color. The image repeats infinitely to the right, while the #dedad1 background color fills in all space not occupied by the image. (See extra bits on page 99.)

4 Set our baseline font color. This will be overwritten for specific components later.

5 Set styling of two of our content header types.

6 Define the width of our page and make it always center horizontally in a browser.

Save the style sheet as onthego.css in the common/css directory.

If you open index.html in a browser, your page should look like this.

code site page

add masthead

Let's add a masthead to our site to give it a little branding.

Add the new code shown below to index.html and then save the file:

```
<div id="container">
  <div id="masthead">
    <img src="img/logo.gif" width="318" height="72"
alt="On The Go Footage" />
  </div>

  <!-- Start Content -->
  <div id="content">

  </div>
  <!-- end content -->
</div>
```

1 Our site's logo with alternate text that will appear in the event images are disabled in the browser. (See extra bits on page 99.)

Now, let's add some CSS to style the masthead. Type the following code at the end of onthego.css and save it when you are finished. (Numbered captions refer to steps on page 82.)

```
/* Masthead
------------------------------- */
#masthead {
  height: 72px;
  margin-bottom: 12px;
  background: url(../../img/bg_masthead.gif) no-repeat 318px 0;
}
```

1 Space between bottom of masthead and content

2 Background image positioned 318 pixels from left

add masthead (cont.)

1 Create a little space between the bottom of the masthead and the content that will follow. (Steps refer to code at the bottom of page 81.)

2 Add the background image and position it 318 pixels from the left, putting it just after the logo.

Refresh your browser with ⌈Ctrl⌉⌈F5⌉ on Windows or ⌈⌘⌉⌈R⌉ on Mac OS X to see the latest version of index.html. Your page should look like this. (See extra bits on page 99.)

add video details

Now we'll add the container for the video player and the details of the video that will be playing, focusing more on the latter for now. We'll show how to do this in two sections of code to better explain how it all gets pieced together.

Let's begin with adding the following code to index.html:

```
<div id="content">
    <!-- Start Video Playing column -->
    <div id="videoPlaying">
        <div id="silverlightControlHost">
        </div>

        </div><!-- end video playing column -->
</div>
<!-- end content -->
```

1 Add the column that will contain both your video player and the playing video's details.

2 Add the container for your Silverlight video player. This will be empty for now, but we will add the video player code later in this chapter.

Now let's style the new content by adding the following code at the end of onthego.css: (Numbered captions refer to steps on page 84.)

```
/* Video Playing column
------------------------------- */
#videoPlaying {
   float: left;
   width: 554px;
}

/* Holds the Silverlight video player */
#videoPlaying #silverlightControlHost {
   width: 512px;
   height: 390px;
}
```

1 Set column alignment and width

2 Set dimensions for video player

code site page   83

add video details (cont.)

1 Situate our column to the left and define its width. (See extra bits on page 100.) (Steps refer to code at the bottom of page 83.)

2 You will recall that when you tested your outputted video player in Chapter 6, it took up the whole browser window even if you resized it. Here you are defining a specific width and height for it so there is room for other content on the page. (See extra bits on page 100.)

Let's add details below the video player about the video that is playing. (You may enter details that are pertinent to your video.)

```
<div id="silverlightControlHost">
</div>

<!-- Start Video Details -->
  <div id="videoDetails">
    <h1>My Trip to South Africa, Part I: The Eagle</h1>

    <p class="info"><strong>From:</strong> sjackson <span>|</span> <strong>Added:</strong> Nov 8, 2008 <span>|</span> <strong>Length:</strong> 00:16</p>
  </div><!-- end video details -->
</div><!-- end video playing column -->
```

1 Add the title of the video that is playing.

2 Add the fictitious name of the user who uploaded the video to the site.

3 Add the date the video was uploaded to the site.

4 Add the video's length.

(See extra bits on page 100.)

Now let's style the new content by adding the following code at the end of onthego.css as usual:

```css
/* Video Details below player */
#videoDetails {
  width: 460px;
  margin-top: 9px;
  padding: 19px 26px 16px;
  background: #e9e6e0;
}

#videoDetails p, #videoDetails label {
  color: #7a7a78;
}

#videoDetails p {
  font-size: 0.8125em;
}

#videoDetails .info {
  margin: 11px 0 13px;
}

#videoDetails span {
  padding-left: 3px;
  padding-right: 3px;
  color: #bebdbb;
}
```

1 Define the video details container width and background color, and provide space above it and padding inside it.

2 Define paragraph and form label font color and paragraph font size within the video details container.

3 Add formatting specific to the paragraph containing the From, Added, and Length video information so there is space above and below it.

4 Format the element containing the bar (|) separating the video information.

We have a couple more video details to add within the videoDetails container in index.html. As before, these details will be different for your video.

add video details (cont.)

```
<p class="info"><strong>From:</strong> sjackson <span>|
</span> <strong>Added:</strong> Feb 20, 2008 <span>|</span>
<strong>Length:</strong> 00:16</p>

<form action="">
  <fieldset>
    <label for="url">Share video URL:</label> <input type="text"
id="url" value="http://www.onthegofootage.com/index.html" />
  </fieldset>
</form>

<p class="description">We spotted an eagle perched in a tree,
and much to our delight, we saw it swoop down to the water in
front of us and back up again.</p>
</div><!-- end video details -->
```

1 Add the URL value for the page you are building. This will allow your site's users to copy the URL and paste it into an email or instant message to share the video page with friends. (See extra bits on page 100.)

2 Add a brief description of the video.

Let's style this final part of the video details by adding the following code at the end of onthego.css as usual:

```
#videoDetails .description {
  width: 447px;
  margin-top: 17px;
  padding-top: 19px;
  border-top: 1px solid #b8b5af;
}
```

1 Format the video description, adding the horizontal line via a border at the top.

```
#videoDetails input {
  width: 343px;
  padding: 3px;
  border: 1px solid #a5acb2;
}

#videoDetails input, #videoDetails label {
  font-size: 0.6875em;
  vertical-align: middle;
}

#videoDetails label {
  font-weight: bold;
}
```

2 Format the URL form element.

Test your updates as you have previously. Make sure you have saved both index.html and onthego.css. Refresh your browser with [Ctrl][F5] on Windows or [⌘][R] on Mac OS to see the latest version of the page. Your page should look like this.

The big space between the masthead and the video details will be filled by the video player later in this chapter.

code site page

add more videos list

In addition to featuring a video, our page will contain a list of more videos that might interest the user. (See extra bits on page 100.)

Add this code to index.html: (Numbered captions refer to steps on page 89.)

```
</div><!-- end video playing column -->

<!-- Start More Videos -->
<div id="videos">
    <h2>More Videos</h2>
    <ul>
        <li>
            <img src="img/thumb/thumb_video_02.jpg" width="100"
height="67" alt="" />
            <div>
                <h3><a href="video-02.html">Video 2 Title</a></h3>
                <p>videoGuy <span>|</span> Sep 22, 2008 <span>|
</span> 01:07</p>
            </div>
        </li>
        <li>
            <img src="img/thumb/thumb_video_03.jpg"
width="100" height="67" alt="" />
            <div>
                <h3><a href="video-03.html">Video 3 Title</a></h3>
                <p>adventuregal <span>|</span> Oct 17, 2008 <span>|
</span> 02:32</p>
            </div>
        </li>
    </ul>
</div>
    <!-- end more videos -->

</div>
<!-- end content -->
```

2 More Videos column header

3 Begin unordered list

4 First list element

5 Video link on title text

6 Thumbnail image

7 Name of user, date, and length

8 Next list element

9 End unordered list

1 Add the container for the More Videos column.

code site page

2 Add the More Videos column header. (Steps refer to code on page 88.)

3 Begin the unordered list that contains the videos.

4 Add an `<li></li>` element for each video in the list.

5 Add the thumbnail image. (See extra bits on page 101.)

6 Add a link (represented by `<a href="video-02.html"></a>`) to the video's page on the video's title (represented by the Video 2 Title text in between the `<a></a>`). We are using generic video titles and file names ordered by number to make the example more clear. (See extra bits on page 101.) You will learn how to create these additional video pages in the next chapter.

7 Add the fictitious name of the user who uploaded the video to the site, the date it was uploaded, and its length.

8 Add another video to the list.

9 End the unordered list that contains the videos.

Your list now has two videos in it. Add four more by copying and pasting the `<li></li>` block you entered for Video 3, changing the thumbnail, link, and title numbers incrementally, as well as the user name, date, and video length as desired.

After having done so, your last video in the list will resemble this:

```
      </li>
      <li>
         <img src="img/thumb/thumb_video_07.jpg" width="100"
height="67" alt="" />
         <div>
            <h3><a href="video-07.html">Video 7 Title</a></h3>
            <p>travelfreak <span>|</span> Nov 04, 2008
<span>|< span> 01:05</p>
         </div>
      </li>
   </ul>
</div>
<!-- end more videos -->
```

code site page   **89**

add more videos list (cont.)

OK, now that you have your list content together, add some styling to the end of onthego.css.

```css
/* More Videos List
-------------------------------- */
#videos {
   margin-left: 554px;
}

#videos h2 {
   border-bottom: 3px solid #7e7b76;
   margin-bottom: 0.9em;
   padding-bottom: 0.8125em;
}

#videos li {
   min-height: 67px;
   margin-bottom: 1.25em;
   background: #f0eeea;
}

#videos li:hover {
   background-color: #fff;
}

#videos li img {
   float: left;
}
```

1 Define the margin of the More Videos column container from the left of the content's container.

2 Format each list item so its minimum height is the same as the thumbnail image. (Change this value to the height of your thumbnails if it is different.)

3 Make the background color of the list item change when you hover over it. (Note: This will only display in modern browsers.)

4 Place the thumbnail image to the left of the text in each list item.

code site page

```
#videos li div {
  margin-left: 115px;
  padding: 16px 5px 5px 0;
}

#videos li h3 {
  font-size: 0.8125em;
  font-weight: bold;
}

#videos li p {
  margin-top: 9px;
  font-size: 0.825em;
}

#videos li p span {
  padding-left: 3px;
  padding-right: 3px;
  color: #c6c5c4;
}
```

5 Style the video title and descriptive text.

We have one small adjustment to make for Internet Explorer 6 before we can test our latest changes. Start a new file in your text editor and put only the following CSS in it:

```
/* Styles for Internet Explorer 6
------------------------------------- */

#videos li {
  height: 67px;
}
```

add more videos list (cont.)

Now save the file as onthego_ie6.css in common/css, where onthego.css lives.

This small bit of CSS is required because Internet Explorer 6 does not understand the `min-height` property and because it interprets the `height` property differently than modern browsers. You might recall that when you started the HTML page earlier in this chapter, you entered some code to load a small style sheet to provide rules specific to Internet Explorer 6. This is the file in question, and no other browsers will load it (except for versions of Internet Explorer below or equal to 6).

Let's test your updates. Make sure you have saved index.html, onthego.css, and onthego_ie6.css. Refresh your browser with Ctrl F5 on Windows or ⌘R on Mac OS X to see the latest version of the page. Your page should look like this.—

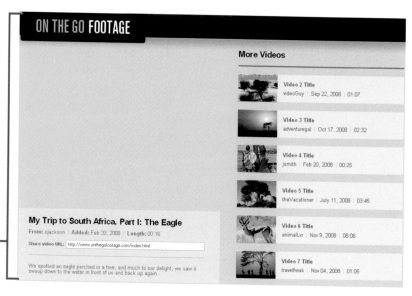

add footer

You are getting close to completing the page. All that remains is adding a page footer and the video player. Let's tackle the footer first.

Add this code to index.html:

```
    </div>
    <!-- end video list -->
  </div>
  <!-- end content -->

  <div id="footer">
    <p>&copy; Copyright 2008 OnTheGoFootage</p>
  </div>
</div>

</body>
</html>
```

1 Add the footer container. (See extra bits on page 101.)

2 Add a copyright symbol (©) and notice.

add footer (cont.)

Now add this to the end of onthego.css:

```css
/* Footer
-------------------------------- */
#footer {
    clear: both;
    margin-top: 25px;
    padding: 7px 10px;
    background-color: #c9c3b6;
}

#footer p {
    font-size: 0.825em;
    color: #7c725e;
}
```

1 Make sure the footer appears on its own line below all page content and give it some simple styling.

2 Format the copyright text.

Let's test your updates once again. Make sure you have saved index.html and onthego.css. Refresh your browser with Ctrl F5 on Windows or ⌘R on Mac OS X to see the latest version of the page. Your page should look like this.

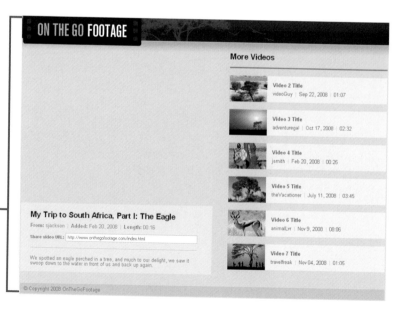

code site page

add video player

Our page is set, and all it needs is your video player.

You will be using the player code that Encoder generated in Default.html when it outputted your video and player.

1 Open Default.html in your text editor.

2 Scroll down to the bottom of the code and copy the entire `<object></object>` element by highlighting it and hitting Ctrl C on Windows or ⌘ C on Mac OS X.

3 Now switch over to index.html and paste the object code inside the silverlightControlHost div by hitting Ctrl V on Windows or ⌘ V on Mac OS X.

```
<!-- Start Video Playing column -->
<div id="videoPlaying">
   <div id="silverlightControlHost">
      <object data="data:application/x-silverlight-2,"
type="application/x-silverlight-2" width="100%" height="100%">
         <param name="source" value="silverlight/MediaPlayerTemplate.xap"/>
         <param name="onerror" value="onSilverlightError" />
         <param name="initparams" value='autoplay=True,
autoload=True,enablecaptions=True,muted=False,stretchmode=0,
displaytimecode=False,playlist=<playList><playListItems>
<playListItem title="The%20Eagle" description="An%20eagle%20
swoops%20down%20toward%20a%20lake%20and%20flies%20to%20a%20
tree." mediaSource="media/video/quickproject_1.wmv"
adaptiveStreaming="False" thumbSource="img/thumb/
quickproject_1_Thumb.jpg" frameRate="29.9676648895841"
width="512" height="344" ><chapters><chapter position="7.220"
thumbnailSource="img/chapter/quickproject_1_7.220.jpg"
title="Chapter%201" /><chapter position="10.500"
thumbnailSource="img/chapter/quickproject_1_10.500.jpg"
title="Chapter%202" /></chapters></playListItem>
</playListItems></playList>' />
```

Continued onto
next page

Continued onto
next page

code site page

95

add video player (cont.)

Continued from
previous page

Continued from
previous page

2

3

```
        <a href="http://go2.microsoft.com/fwlink/?LinkID=124807"
style="text-decoration: none;">
        <img src="http://go2.microsoft.com/
fwlink/?LinkId=108181" alt="Get Microsoft Silverlight"
style="border-style: none"/>
        </a>
      </object>
    </div>
```

Now let's set the background color of our Silverlight object so it matches our page. Without this change, you would see little white areas at each rounded corner of the player.

1 Add a background param in the object element.

```
<param name="onerror" value="onSilverlightError" />
<param name="background" value="#dedad1" />
<param name="initparams"
```

There is a little bit of code worth cleaning up, too. Toward the bottom of the object code you will see:

```
<a href="http://go2.microsoft.com/fwlink/?LinkID=124807"
style="text-decoration: none;">
  <img src="http://go2.microsoft.com/fwlink/?LinkId=108181"
alt="Get Microsoft Silverlight" style="border-style: none"/>
</a>
```

code site page

This is the Install Microsoft Silverlight image and link that shows if the user does not have the plug-in installed in his or her browser. (See extra bits on page 102.)

As you can see, there is some inline CSS (highlighted in the code above), as defined by style="". You learned earlier that it is a best practice to keep your content (that is to say, HTML) separate from your presentation (that is to say, CSS), so we don't want to leave these styles in the HTML. Normally we would move them to our style sheet, but fortunately, onthego.css already defines these rules, so we can simply remove them from the HTML.

1 Change the install code so the inline styles are removed, as shown:

```
<a href="http://go2.microsoft.com/fwlink/?LinkID=124807">
  <img src="http://go2.microsoft.com/fwlink/?LinkId=108181"
alt="Get Microsoft Silverlight" />
</a>
```

Alright, you're all done! Let's test the fruits of your labor. Make sure you have saved index. html and onthego. css. Refresh your browser with Ctrl F5 on Windows or ⌘ R on Mac OS X to see the latest version of the page. (See extra bits on page 102.) Your page should look like this, with your video playing back automatically.

extra bits

gather assets p. 74

- It is a best practice not to repeat the image type (thumb, in this case) in the file name if its folder name represents the same. In other words, it is redundant to have a thumb_ image in a thumb folder. However, we've done so here to be explicit and make the code example a little easier to follow.

start HTML page p. 76

- We are using the XHTML 1.0 Strict DOCTYPE for our code. The W3C provides a service at http:// validator.w3.org/#validate-by-upload to help you make sure your code is valid. Invalid code often still works, but it is a good practice to validate your code, and it may help you catch any typing errors during our exercise. It should be noted that once you put the video player object code from Encoder into your page toward the end of in this chapter, your code will no longer validate. That is OK in this instance. For more information about XHTML 1.0, consult http:// www.w3.org/TR/xhtml1/ or an HTML reference.

start style sheet p. 78

- Whereas HTML provides the content for a page, CSS dictates the presentation. You may have seen CSS placed inline in HTML, but it is a best practice to keep content and presentation separated in the manner we are doing.

- Web browsers have default style settings (such as margins and padding) on various HTML elements. However, they aren't always consistent from one browser to the next. A CSS Reset is a CSS rule or series of rules aimed at establishing a consistent baseline amongst browsers upon which you can then build your page. We are using a simplified version of Eric Meyer's CSS Reset (see http://meyerweb.com/eric/ thoughts/2007/05/01/reset-reloaded/). This is just one of a few approaches, though his is one of the most widely adopted. Perform a search for css resets if you are interested in seeing more.

- Hexadecimal color declarations are not case-sensitive, meaning that #dedad1, #DEDAD1 and #dEDaD1 (or any similar variation) all render the same. You will often see the all-caps approach used. The choice is just a matter of one's personal preference. Whichever direction you choose, it's best to be consistent for code legibility.

- We are using relative paths to reference background images from CSS. The path to an image is relative to where the style sheet is located in your folder structure. In our case, it is located in common/css, so in order to reference the image, the URL path must point up two directory levels to the site root, and down one into the img folder, hence url(../../img/bg.gif).

add masthead p. 81

- Some developers advocate surrounding a site's logo with the <h1></h1> HTML element, and there is plenty of healthy discussion about both approaches (with it and without it) online. We are advocating here as a best practice to use the h1 for the most important header within the content area instead of the logo, as that is more likely to change from page to page and be more meaningful to search engines as a result (though search engines do not reveal their algorithms explicitly). Furthermore, a search engine will already know what site it is on, as reinforced by the title text.

- If you don't see your changes, double-check that you saved both index.html and onthego.css in your editor. If you still don't see your changes, clear your browser cache and reload the page again.

- To simplify the example, we used an <img /> element to add the logo to the page. A second approach (arguably better) is to use a CSS image replacement technique. An example is available on the companion site.

extra bits (cont.)

add video details p. 83

- The videoPlaying column is wider than the content within it (such as the player) in order to create space between it and the moreVideos column that will be added to the right later in this chapter.

- You may have noticed that the width and height of our player container is different than the width and height of the encoded video itself. The container's width and height needs to account for the player's chrome and buttons, hence the different dimensions. You can change these dimensions to fit your particular needs. It may require some trial and error to find the width and height you like best.

- The video details information could be structured in at least a couple ways. For instance, one might suggest an HTML definition list would be appropriate.

- Be sure to customize the URL value to match your site. Our example shows the URL as http://www.onthegofootage.com/index.html. Replace the value with your domain and page name (if you are not calling it index.html). For instance, your URL value might be http://www.mydomainnamehere.com/scary-clown.html for a page featuring a video of a birthday party gone awry.

add more videos list p. 88

- You may have noticed that Encoder has player templates that include a gallery of videos. That is, a video player with a list of other videos that can be played, too. So, why not use that in our page instead? One reason is that by placing the list of more videos in HTML, search engines will index your video content and increase the likelihood of your site being found via a Web search. Secondly, an HTML videos list provides you flexibility over what kind of content you want to appear in it and how you want it to appear instead of being beholden to what the Encoder template dictates. (Note that you can modify or create a player template. See the appendix for more details.) Additionally, it is far easier to update the videos list if it is in HTML. By contrast, in Encoder you would need to import all of the videos you wanted to appear in the list, apply the necessary presets, select the player template, and perform an encode.

code site page

- Our example uses the sample thumbnails provided in the ZIP file you downloaded from the companion site. Replace the thumbnail name with your own if you have outputted additional videos from Encoder.
- While our example uses generic video page and title names, it is, of course, best to make them descriptive of the content. They will be more meaningful to both your site's users and search engines. So, instead of Video 2 Title, your video title might be Footrace through the Sahara and you could name the file containing the video footrace-through-sahara.html. The title and name do not have to be the same, but it stands to reason that they should be similar.

add footer p. 93

- Note that the footer could be accomplished solely with a paragraph element instead of surrounding it with a `<div></div>` container. However, by using the div, you may add more content to the footer, such as links to a terms of use and privacy policy page, or other ancillary information on your site.

extra bits (cont.)

add video player p. 95

- You can customize what the user sees when they do not have the plug-in by replacing this default install image with something of your choosing.

- When you test your page, you may get a message from your browser indicating that for security reasons it is restricting the page from showing active content. It is referring to the Silverlight content, which in this case is not a security risk. This message only appears when testing the page locally (that is to say, from your hard drive) and not when your code is deployed on your Web server. It is OK to allow the browser to show blocked content. After doing so, you will see the page refresh and the player load as part of it.

9. create more video pages

So, you have a fully coded, designed, functional video player page for OnTheGoFootage. As a final step, let's learn how to create similar pages for the videos in the More Videos list so users can watch them all. (See extra bits on page 111.)

In this chapter you will:

Create a new video page based on the one from Chapter 8.

Update the new page's More Videos list to include the video from the first page.

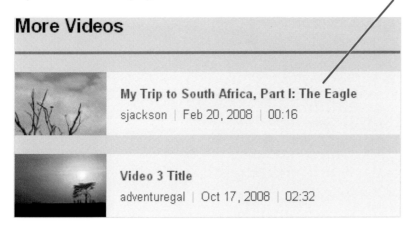

copy page

Your new page will use index.html as a starting point, and then you will customize it for the page's video.

1 In the site directory, copy and paste index.html to make a duplicate of it.

2 Name the new file video-02.html.

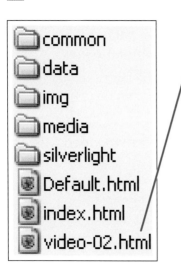

You will recall that when you coded the More Videos list in index.html, the link to the first video in the list was represented as:

```
<a href="video-02.html">Video 2 Title</a>
```

Because you just named your new page video-02.html, when users on index.html click the first link in the list, they will see your new page.

Next, you'll begin to customize video-02.html.

update video details

Let's update video-02.html so it includes details specific to the page's video.

Open video-02.html in your text editor and change the title as shown (see extra bits on page 111.). You will recall that this is the title that shows at the top left of the browser, not the one within the page itself:

```
<head>
<title>Video 02 Title - On The Go Footage</title>
<meta http-equiv="Content-type" content="text/html;
charset=utf-8" />
```

1 Customize browser title for second video page. (Use your own video title as appropriate.)

Now, let's update the video details area.

```
<!-- Start Video Details -->
<div id="videoDetails">
<h1>Video 02 Title</h1>

  <p class="info"><strong>From:</strong> videoGuy
<span>|</span> <strong>Added:</strong> Sep 22, 2008 <span>|
</span> <strong>Length:</strong> 01:07</p>
```

1 Update video title that shows below the player.

2 Update fictitious user who added the second video.

3 Update the date the second video was added.

4 Update the length according to the second video's duration.

update video details (cont.)

The video page's URL and description are the final parts of the details to update.

```
<form action="">
  <fieldset>
    <label for="url">Share video URL:</label> <input type="text"
id="url" value="http://www.onthegofootage.com/video-02.html" />
  </fieldset>
</form>

<p class="description">Your description for video 2.</p>
</div><!-- end video details -->
```

1 Update the URL value so it reflects the new page's name.

2 Update the description for the second video.

When you are finished, the video details area will resemble the figure shown.

Video 2 Title

From: videoGuy | Added: Sep 22, 2008 | Length: 01:07

Share video URL: http://www.onthegofootage.com/video-02.html

Your description for video 2.

update video player

Now let's update the video player object so it shows the second video.

There are two ways you can go about this: For the first way, if you outputted a video player with your second video, then you can copy the `<object></object>` element from that video's Default.html, paste it into video-02.html (replacing the `<object></object>` that is currently there), and make the asset path updates you learned about in Chapter 7. For the second way, you can edit the `<object></object>` in video-02.html directly.

What follows is the second approach so you will know how to perform either method per your preference. In the example that follows, we will assume your video does not have chapters. (See extra bits on page 111.)

1 In video-02.html, look for the chapters code block in the `<object></object>` element.

```
<chapters><chapter position="7.220" thumbnailSource=
"img/chapter/quickproject_1_7.220.jpg" title="Chapter%201" />
<chapter position="10.500" thumbnailSource="img/chapter/
quickproject_1_10.500.jpg" title="Chapter%202" /></chapters>
```

2 Remove the entire chapters block so your `<object></object>` now looks like the following:

```
<object data="data:application/x-silverlight-2,"
type="application/x-silverlight-2" width="100%" height="100%">
   <param name="source" value="silverlight/MediaPlayerTemplate.xap"/>
   <param name="onerror" value="onSilverlightError" />
   <param name="background" value="#dedad1" />
```

Continued onto
next page

update video player (cont.)

Continued from
previous page

2

```
    <param name="initparams" value='autoplay=True,autoload=True,
enablecaptions=True,muted=False,stretchmode=0,displaytimecode
=False,playlist=<playList><playListItems><playListItem title=
"The%20Eagle" description="An%20eagle%20swoops%20down%20
toward%20a%20lake%20and%20flies%20to%20a%20tree."
mediaSource="media/video/quickproject_1.wmv"
adaptiveStreaming="False" thumbSource="img/thumb/
quickproject_1_Thumb.jpg" frameRate="29.9676648895841"
width="512" height="344" ></playListItem></playListItems>
</playList>' />
    <a href="http://go2.microsoft.com/fwlink/?LinkID=124807">
      <img src="http://go2.microsoft.com/fwlink/?LinkId=108181"
alt="Get Microsoft Silverlight" />
    </a>
</object>
```

Now, let's update the playlist portion of the `<object></object>` code so it is customized for the second video. (See extra bits on page 111.)

```
<playList><playListItems><playListItem title="Video 2 Title"
description="Your description for video 2."
mediaSource="media/video/video_02.wmv" adaptiveStreaming=
"False" thumbSource="img/thumb/thumb_video_02.jpg"
frameRate="29.9676648895841" width="512" height="344"
></playListItem></playListItems></playList>
```

1 Update the title and description metadata. This is the metadata you entered in Encoder in Chapter 4, though it likely matches the title and description you are using for the second video in the page too.

2 Update the name of the video file.

3 Update the name of the video thumbnail.

create more video pages

update more videos list

The final update video-02.html needs is to the More Videos list.

Now that Video 2 is playing in the page, it doesn't need to be in the list. Conversely, your first video from index.html is not accessible to users from this page because it isn't in the list. So, let's replace Video 2 with the first one.

In video-02.html, update the first list item with information from the first video.

```
<!-- Start More Videos List -->
<div id="videos">
  <h2>More Videos</h2>
  <ul>
    <li>
          <img src="img/thumb/quickproject_1_Thumb.jpg"
width="100" height="67" alt="" />
        <div>
          <h3><a href="index.html">
My Trip to South Africa, Part I: The Eagle</a></h3>
              <p>sjackson <span>|</span> Feb 20, 2008 <span>|</span>
00:16</p>
        </div>
      </li>
      <li>
```

1 Update the thumbnail image file name for the first video.

2 Update the link file name to reflect the page containing the first video.

3 Update the video title so it matches the first video.

4 Update the fictitious user who added the first video.

5 Update the date the first video was added.

6 Update the length according to the first video's duration.

update more videos list (cont.)

When you are finished, the More Videos list will resemble the figure shown.

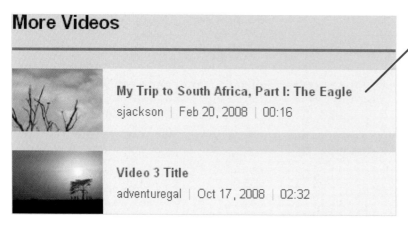

More Videos

My Trip to South Africa, Part I: The Eagle
sjackson | Feb 20, 2008 | 00:16

Video 3 Title
adventuregal | Oct 17, 2008 | 02:32

With that, you have successfully finished a second page. Make sure you save video-02.html.

If you still have index.html open in your browser, click Video 2 Title in the More Videos list to load your second page. Then try going back to the first video by clicking My Trip to South Africa, Part I: The Eagle in the More Videos list of video-02.html.

Repeat the steps shown in this chapter to create pages for additional videos, and you will soon have a completed site ready for uploading. (See extra bits on page 112.)

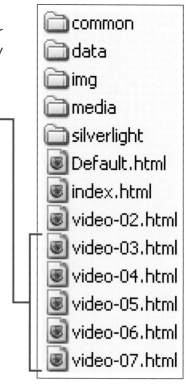

common
data
img
media
silverlight
Default.html
index.html
video-02.html
video-03.html
video-04.html
video-05.html
video-06.html
video-07.html

extra bits

intro p. 103

- Video sites use a couple of approaches to show a video after a user has clicked it from a list of videos. One is to load a new page that contains the selected video. The second is to use JavaScript to tell the video player to play the selected video and update information on the page related to it, all without loading a new page. Our example uses the former approach, in part because at the time of this writing, you can't communicate with the Silverlight 2 video players exported by Encoder 2 SP1 via JavaScript. However, even if that functionality were available, we would still recommend as a best practice to create individual pages for each video, as you will be doing so in this chapter. This allows visitors who do not have JavaScript enabled to still use the site, and it means that a user coming into your site from a search engine result will land on the page featuring the right video. If you were to later layer on the JavaScript-enabled experience, then you would get the best of both worlds. This layering approach is known as Progressive Enhancement. For those interested, a Web search on the topic will yield further definition.

update video details p. 105

- For search engine optimization, try to keep the entire title text within about 65 characters, including spaces and punctuation.

update video player p. 107

- You may find the other approach—outputting a player with each video, and copying and updating its `<object></object>` element—is the easier for you, particularly if your video has chapters. You can update chapters by hand in approach two, but it requires a little more care.

- You will notice that the frameRate, and the video width and height are also defined in the playlist. These may be different for your video. The width and height, as you have seen, is indicated in Encoder when you are making your encoding settings. You may be able to reuse a frameRate in multiple videos, but you can obtain the exact frameRate for each video by outputting a player template with each video and copying the value from Default.html.

extra bits (cont.)

update more videos list p.109

- Your site can have a different number of videos than what has been shown in the More Videos list. Simply add or remove list items as needed. However, if the list is too long, the page will be less usable for users and will lose some of its visual appeal due to being unbalanced. At such a time, you could consider adding numerical links above or below the list that would point to additional pages.

10. publish your site

You have built your site, and now all that is left to do is to upload your files to your Web server and make sure it all works.

upload files

1 Take a final check through your folders to be sure all files are in place. (Note that you will not need to upload either the data folder or Default.html, since neither is used by the site. You can move those somewhere outside the site directory for archiving.)

- site
- common/css
- img
- img/chapter
- img/thumb
- media/video

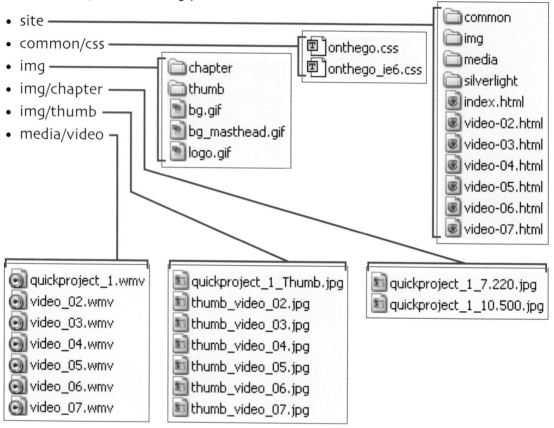

2 Once you are certain you have all the files you will need, you are ready to upload the folders and files using your FTP application. (See extra bits on page 116.) Consult the instructions your Web hosting company provided for logging into your server and transferring files.

3 When you are done uploading the files, open your site in a browser and navigate around to make sure all pages and videos are working as expected.

That's it! You have successfully learned to enhance and encode your video with Encoder, output a Silverlight 2 video player, and build a video site around it.

extra bits

upload files p. 114

- Note that you should not upload
  the site folder itself, just the
  specified files and folders within it.

appendix: additional features

This appendix touches on a handful of features that reach beyond the Encoder essentials you learned during the course of the project.

We provide them here simply to make you aware of additional options, whether they are in Encoder or the greater ecosystem of delivering Silverlight video experiences.

customize video player

It is possible to customize the look and feel of the video player templates Encoder outputs, allowing you to style a player to match your site's brand. You may also save this custom template for future use.

Expression Blend 2 is the primary design tool for creating Silverlight layouts, vector graphics, animations, and transformations. As such, you can use it to customize a player template. You can also modifiy a template in Visual Studio.

Encoder provides easy integration with these tools via clicking the small white box to the right of the template menu.

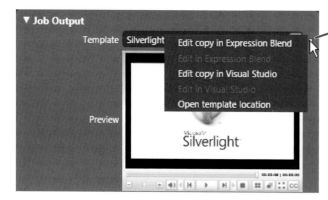

To learn more, see:

- Customize an Expression Encoder template for Silverlight 2 located at http://msdn.microsoft.com/en-us/library/dd185498.aspx.
- The User Guide under Encode your video for Microsoft Silverlight and the Web > Create templates from existing Silverlight players (advanced).

live encoding

Encoder has a Live Encoding Mode that allows you to encode a feed in real time, such as for a concert.

When you enter the mode via the Live encoding button, Encoder switches its interface to the Live encoding workspace. Among other things, the workspace allows you to mix your live feed from a video camera and other devices with preshot videos you have stored.

You can learn more about it in the User Guide under Live Encoding.

batch encoding

If you want to encode several videos at a time, you certainly could import them into Encoder and follow encoding steps similar to what you learned in this book.

However, encoding videos via its GUI is only one way you can take advantage of Encoder. Its encoding engine is also available through the Encoder Object Model (OM) and the command line. What this means is you can generate your own applications or processes to encode videos.

Why might this be helpful? Imagine you were running a site like OnTheGoFootage, to which users were regularly uploading video. Aside from not wanting to place the encoding burden on your users before they upload videos, you want to control the encoding quality of the videos before they are posted on your site.

Certainly, you wouldn't want to manually encode each video with Encoder as it was uploaded. Instead, you could save your encoding settings as a preset and export them from Encoder as an XML file. Your application or process could use that file and run periodically, leveraging Encoder's engine to encode batches of uploaded videos.

More information is available in the User Guide under Software development kit (SDK) and Command-line operation.

iis smooth streaming

Smooth Streaming is an adaptive media streaming technology that adjusts the video quality sent to a Silverlight player as one's bandwidth and local PC conditions fluctuate. It does so without interrupting playback.

Microsoft introduced IIS Smooth Streaming support as part of Encoder 2 SP1 in anticipation of the Media Pack extension it intends to make available for Microsoft Internet Information Services (IIS) in the first quarter of 2009.

To learn more, see:

- http://www.iis.net/media
- The User Guide under Encode your video for Microsoft Silverlight and the Web > Adaptive streaming.

silverlight streaming

Silverlight Streaming is a hosting service provided by Microsoft for serving Silverlight applications and media files, including video. You do not need to use this service to host your Silverlight video player. Any Web hosting service will work.

At the time of this writing, the service was in beta and was free, though with certain limitations in allowed storage, streaming bandwidth, and video length and bit rate. Please note that Silverlight Streaming does not provide live or on-demand video streaming, such as a Windows Media server does. Instead, it delivers videos via progressive download.

There is a plug-in available for Encoder to facilitate publishing to the service. The Silverlight Streaming Publishing Plug-In for Expression Encoder is located at http://www.microsoft.com/downloads/details.aspx?FamilyID=382a3306-b212-4df3-af86-5d48be550b94&displaylang=en.

To learn more about the service, see the Silverlight Streaming SDK at http://msdn.microsoft.com/en-us/library/bb851621.aspx or visit http://silverlight.live.com/.

index

index

index

index